Advance
A Handbook for
An Ignatian Guide
Discernment , ___ ヽ VVIII

This highly practical and lucidly written book is yet another example of why Father Timothy M. Gallagher, O.M.V., is America's preeminent interpreter of and writer on Ignatian spiritual direction and discernment.—**Harvey D, Egan, S.J., Emeritus Professor of Systematic and Mystical Theology, Boston College**

I have used Fr. Timothy M. Gallagher's work on Ignatian discernment for both personal reflection and teaching, from the undergraduate to the doctoral levels. He has established himself as the one of the premier interpreters of Saint Ignatius of Loyola writing in English today, and this book is no exception. A beautiful example of profoundly pastoral theology, *A Handbook for Spiritual Directors: An Ignatian Guide for Accompanying Discernment of God's Will* offers an important complement to his earlier work *Discerning the Will of God: An Ignatian Guide to Christian Decision Making*, which has been a source of consolation for many today who seek guidance from Ignatius's wisdom about discernment. This new book will be a *sine qua non* for the training of spiritual directors, especially as interest in Ignatian discernment grows at retreat centers, parishes, and universities worldwide. I am grateful for the important work that Fr. Gallagher has undertaken and for the many who will benefit from his work. —**Tim Muldoon, author of *The Ignatian Workout* and *Living against the Grain: How to Make Decisions that Lead to an Authentic Life***

A wonderful book! Sure to become a standard text for those in ministry. It will be an invaluable resource for all spiritual directors and those in pastoral ministry. Simply put, Gallagher "gets" St. Ignatius of Loyola. He understands Loyola's timeless wisdom and effectively teaches the reader to understand it as well.—**Mark E. Thibodeaux, S.J., spiritual director and author of *Armchair Mystic* and *God, I Have Issues***

The fruit of mature reflection and prayer, Fr. Timothy Gallagher's book, aimed specifically at assisting those who help others to discern the will of God, has been eagerly awaited by spiritual directors. With the hallmark of his earlier work Gallagher employs pertinent existential experiences to illustrate and concretize his points and helpful scriptural readings for prayer. Importantly, the work exemplifies the dispositions that Gallagher seeks to inculcate not just in would-be "discerners" but also and significantly in the directors themselves. These involve a maturity and disciplined practice regarding prayer, both meditation and contemplation; faithfulness to making the examen; the review of prayer and attending to repetition; and an ongoing conscious employment of the rules for discernment. The goal is to be so well disposed that openness to the will of God becomes a deep fissure within. Though the aim is to assist the "discerner," spiritual directors know well that they are blessed in and through the process. This work makes clear our challenge is to be deeply honed instruments for such service! — **Gill Goulding, C.J., Professor of Systematic Theology, Regis College, Toronto**

Certain qualities are required in any handbook such as this. It needs to be based on sound scholarship and, as a result, to be dependable. But it must also be intelligible and user-friendly, especially for less scholarly or less experienced spiritual directors who come to rely on it. Gallagher's work has these positive qualities and many more. He is painstaking in making ideas accessible, patient in teasing out the meaning of the technical words (e.g., consolation, desolation, review) that Ignatius uses, and meticulous in tracing the dynamic of the different "modes" of discernment. Because of its clarity the book makes easy reading, but this is not to say that it allows for a quick reading. On almost every page there are issues raised that will give the reader (especially a spiritual director) pause. These passages will provoke deep reflection on the reader's own personal experience of decision making, as well as on those occasions when they accompanied others in their search for the will of God. Gallagher demands high standards in the spiritual director. Expect to feel uneasy at times! — **Brian O'Leary, S.J., writer and retreat director, Dublin, Ireland**

Advance Praise

Fr. Timothy Gallagher has succeeded in writing an important and very useful sequel to his *Discerning the Will of God: An Ignatian Guide to Christian Decision Making*. It is addressed especially to spiritual directors who may be journeying with someone who is discerning God's will in their life. Spiritual directors will find important, practical examples and settings to help them in the indispensable ministry of accompanying someone discerning God's will outside the context of the "full" Spiritual Exercises. —**Ernest Sherstone, O.M.V., Founder of the Lanteri Center for Ignatian Spirituality, Denver, and director of St. Joseph Retreat House, Milton, MA**

Spiritual directors and those who form them will find a treasure in Fr. Timothy Gallagher's book, *A Handbook for Spiritual Directors: An Ignatian Guide for Accompanying Discernment of God's Will*. Fr. Gallagher's careful study of classical texts have brought clarity and depth to the understanding of Ignatian discernment. He facilitates a transfer of wisdom from these first spiritual directors to contemporary ones who are asking similar questions about the faithful accompaniment of those who truly desire to choose God's will. Accessible, thoughtful, and pastorally sensitive, this book is sure to be a lasting resource for teachers and directors alike. —**Catherine Macaulay, spiritual director, wife, and mother, faculty of the Ignatian Centre, Montreal**

It is one thing to understand St. Ignatius's teaching on discerning the will of God, and quite another to understand how to apply that teaching in guiding particular persons in vocational discernment. Fr. Gallagher draws on his many years of study and experience to provide a practical guidebook for those privileged to accompany others in discerning the will of God. This book has strengthened my confidence as a spiritual director. —**Daniel P. Barron, O.M.V., Director of Spiritual Formation, St. John Vianney Theological Seminary, Denver, CO**

Fr. Gallagher gives spiritual directors the insight and tools needed to help others to lay the foundation for discerning the will of God, to remove the human and spiritual obstacles to discovering it, and

Advance Praise

to form the proper disposition of heart for cooperating with it. This handbook offers wise and practical help for all who accompany others in the spiritual life. —**Christina Lynch, Ph.D., Director of Psychological Services, St. John Vianney Theological Seminary, Denver, CO**

In this handbook for spiritual directors, Timothy Gallagher, O.M.V., has made the process of spiritual discernment come alive. His explanations are clear and help to demystify the elements of the discernment process in the Spiritual Exercises of St. Ignatius. This book is an important reference for spiritual directors who accompany others as they reflect on and make important decisions. Thank you Fr. Gallagher for producing this valuable resource. —**Elizabeth Koessler, spiritual director, wife, and mother, faculty of the Ignatian Centre, Montreal**

Fr. Gallagher provides a much-needed handbook that supports spiritual directors in accompanying others through St. Ignatius's classic guidelines for spiritual decision making. He is a sure guide who leads us with clarity and helpful precision through Ignatian terminology and method. Always faithful to the mind of Ignatius, Fr. Gallagher supplements the original laconic text by helping to answer many of the questions that we may have wanted to ask Ignatius. This is an eminently useful reference book, full of illuminating insights and practical suggestions. —**Paul Empsall, spiritual director, faculty of the Ignatian Centre, Montreal**

A Handbook
for
Spiritual Directors

Also by Timothy M. Gallagher, O.M.V.

Praying the Liturgy of the Hours
A Personal Journey

Begin Again
The Life and Spiritual Legacy of Bruno Lanteri

A Reader's Guide to the Discernment of Spirits

Discerning the Will of God
An Ignatian Guide to Christian Decision Making

Meditation and Contemplation
An Ignatian Guide to Praying with Scripture

Spiritual Consolation
An Ignatian Guide for the Greater Discernment of Spirits

An Ignatian Introduction to Prayer
Spiritual Reflections According to the Spiritual Exercises

The Examen Prayer
Ignatian Wisdom for Our Lives Today

The Discernment of Spirits
An Ignatian Guide for Everyday Living

A Handbook
for
Spiritual Directors

An Ignatian Guide for Accompanying
Discernment of God's Will

TIMOTHY M. GALLAGHER, O.M.V.

A Crossroad Book
The Crossroad Publishing Company
Chestnut Ridge, New York

The Crossroad Publishing Company
831 Chestnut Ridge Road
Chestnut Ridge, NY 10977

www.crossroadpublishing.com

Library of Congress Cataloging-in-Publication Data
available from the Library of Congress.

ISBN 978-0-8245-2171-4

Contents

Acknowledgments

I am deeply grateful to the many who have assisted me in the writing of this book, in particular: to those who read and offered comments on the manuscript, Father Daniel Barron, O.M.V., Father Harvey Egan, S.J., Paul Empsall, Father Richard Gabuzda, Claire-Marie Hart, Elizabeth Koessler, Dr. Christina Lynch, Cathie Macaulay, Richard McKinney, and Father Ernest Sherstone, O.M.V.; to Carol McGinness for her invaluable aid with the practicalities of publication; to Sister Bernadette Reis, F.S.P., for her helpful counsel with technical issues regarding publication; to Roy Carlisle whose contributions as editor greatly benefitted this book; and to Gwendolin Herder, president, Christy Korrow, and all at Crossroad Publishing who supported this book from its inception through publication: for what is now a long-standing and consistently positive relationship, I express my sincere thanks.

Finally, I thank the following for permission to reprint copyrighted material:

Excerpts from the Catholic Edition of the Revised Standard Version of the Bible, copyright 1965, 1966 by the Division of Christian Education of the National Council of the Churches of Christ in the United States of America. Used by permission. All rights reserved.

Excerpts from *Discerning God's Will: Ignatius of Loyola's Teaching on Christian Decision Making,* by Jules Toner, S.J., 1991. Chestnut Hill, MA: Institute of Jesuit Sources, 2016. Used by permission.

Excerpts from *Moving in the Spirit: Becoming a Contemplative in Action,* by Richard Hauser, S.J., 1986. Copyright @ 1986 by Paulist Press, Inc., New York/Mahwah, NJ. Used with permission of Paulist Press. www.paulistpress.com.

INTRODUCTION

When Asked to Help Discern God's Will

"I am facing an important choice in my life, and I want to do God's will. I am not sure, however, which option God wants. Can you help me discern God's will in this matter?" Spiritual directors receive few requests more demanding than this. They know the responsibility they accept in accompanying such discernment: the choices such persons make will shape their lives in significant ways and often affect many others.

Directors may or may not feel equipped to accept such requests. Even experienced directors may wish for clearer guidelines on how to proceed. In the process of discernment, they may encounter situations that leave them unsure: Can I invite this person to begin discernment now, or is preparation needed first? How can I help this person prepare? We have begun the discernment, and months are passing . . . but no clarity has emerged: What is missing? Have I overlooked something? Is the person resisting the process? Incapable of making a commitment? The person now feels that the choice is clear, but I as director am less sure, and I wonder: Should I accept this person's sense of clarity? Are there further steps we should employ? What should I as director do in these circumstances?

Over the centuries, directors have faced these questions, and our tradition has provided them answers. The primary exponent of this tradition is Ignatius of Loyola, whose particular gift was clear counsel in matters of discernment: the discernment of spirits and the discernment of God's will in choices we face. This teaching is found in Ignatius's *Spiritual Exercises* and further clarified in his other writings and personal witness. Through the years, commentators have explored this teaching and supplied advice to directors for its application.

Eight years ago, I wrote a book on discerning God's will. That book was directed to the person discerning.[1] In it, I sought to render Ignatius's teaching on discernment accessible for such persons, to help them prepare and then discern. That book discussed the different choices discerners face, the foundation on which sound discernment must be built, the disposition necessary for discernment, the spiritual means to be employed, Ignatius's classic three modes of discernment and how to apply them,[2] when to conclude the process, and its fruits. Throughout, the presence of a director was presumed.

That book arose both from extensive research and from decades of experience. The study focused first of all on Ignatius's own writing on discernment.[3] It also incorporated contemporary authors and, in particular, Jules Toner's excellent writing on discerning God's will.[4] It explored the works of skilled Jesuit directors of the sixteenth century, many trained by Ignatius himself, among them Diego Miró, Juan Alfonso de Polanco, Gil González Dávila, Fabio de Fabi, Antonio Cordeses, and the Official Directory of 1599.[5] It focused also on the Spanish Jesuit masters of the past century, Ignacio Iparraguirre, José Calveras, Ignacio Casanovas, Candido de Dalmases, Eusebio Hernández, and Daniel Gil, to name only a few.[6]

As I read, a conviction grew that another book on discerning God's will was needed, this time for the director who accompanies the process—the original addressee of Ignatius's teaching. In these sources, I encountered a pastoral wisdom that answered with unparalleled precision questions of the kind raised above. I learned that the tradition has addressed the questions directors face today and answered them with depth of insight.

At the same time, I perceived that this wisdom is not readily accessible today. For the most part, it remains locked in writings of the past. Much of it was written in other languages and remains untranslated into English. My persuasion that a bridge was needed grew.

Directors called to accompany another's discernment, if they are to employ Ignatius's teaching well, need practical counsel. They need it in detail. They need answers to the questions expressed above if they are to guide discernment responsibly.

This wisdom, I realized, did not need to be recreated. It already existed in the tradition. It did need, however, to be retrieved and re-presented in view of contemporary cultural conditions. Such is the goal of this book: to gather the best wisdom of the Ignatian tradition regarding discernment of God's will and offer spiritual directors a handbook, a clear and usable tool, for applying this teaching today.[7] Its purpose is to digest the pastoral wisdom found in the sources named and, in the light of decades of experience, my own and that of other directors, create the practical tool described.

This is a book for spiritual directors. In it I presume that readers possess the formation requisite for spiritual direction: personal experience of prayer and discernment, an understanding of spiritual direction as distinct from therapy and pastoral counseling, a basic grounding in Scripture and theology, an adequate nonprofessional familiarity with psychological issues, the necessary listening skills, and so forth. Consequently, I will not repeat these fundamentals.

Since this book explores Ignatian discernment of God's will, I also presume directors who know the Ignatian way or are willing to learn it. Obviously, for example, directors cannot help discerners apply Ignatius's rules for discernment unless they know them well. In earlier books, I have explored in depth these Ignatian elements—his two sets of rules for the discernment of spirits, his examen prayer, and his approach to prayer with Scripture.[8] In this book, I can only provide a summary of these spiritual tools, a brief refresher for those familiar with them and for others a taste of what must be learned if they wish to guide Ignatian discernment of God's will. For a complete discussion of these elements, therefore, I refer readers to these earlier books. Assuming a basic knowledge of these elements, the present book will show how to employ them in accompanying discernment of God's will.

This handbook may be used both in and outside the formal Spiritual Exercises. When directors accompany discernment of God's will within the Spiritual Exercises, whether in retreat houses or in daily life,[9] this book provides them a tool for applying Ignatius's wisdom to the retreatant's discernment. This, obviously, is an ideal setting for discernment and a blessing whenever possible.

Many discernments, however, must be made outside the Spiritual

Exercises. Often the person discerning may have no freedom to make a formal retreat. Likewise, many discernments arise in life, and retreats most often cannot be made to respond to them. Many decisions, too, must be made in limited amounts of time, as, for example, when a person must reply to a job offer in a specified number of weeks. In these and parallel cases, the elements of Ignatian discernment, appropriately adapted to the situation, will help directors to accompany discernment of God's will. Ignatius's teaching will provide the difference between groping for a way to guide the discernment and following a proven path with precise spiritual means.

"There is no doubt," writes one Ignatian master, "that the mind and aim of St. Ignatius is that the three modes of discernment [given in the *Spiritual Exercises*] should also guide many acts of life, until they become an ordinary way of proceeding in life."[10] Ignatius himself applied his modes of discernment to decisions in daily life.[11] When director and directee employ them in such discernments, they will know that they are walking a sure road toward discernment.

Limiting this book to a single issue—discerning God's will in significant choices—permits us to explore such discernment in depth. We will examine in detail the entire process of discernment from its preparation to its conclusion. In particular, we will explore Ignatius's three modes of discernment with careful attention to his text and an abundance of examples. Our perspective throughout will be the spiritual director's role in applying this teaching.

Some of the examples given are found in published sources; many derive from personal interviews with the author. In each case, I share these with the explicit permission of the person. In relating their stories, I have changed the names and some exterior details to preserve the privacy of the speakers. The experiences themselves, however, are recounted exactly as these persons described them. To all who shared in this way, I am profoundly grateful.[12]

My aim in this book, as in earlier books, is to allow the original texts to speak directly. For that reason, I have translated these texts, those of Ignatius himself and the various commentaries, as they were written. Readers will note the consistent use of the masculine in these texts, both in my translations and in those of other publications I will quote. I reproduce this usage out of fidelity to the originals but, obviously, without any intention of limiting their application. The teaching contained in them applies without distinction to all directors who wish to learn and employ Ignatian discernment.

Over the years, commentators have interpreted differently various points of Ignatius's teaching on discerning God's will. In view of the sensitivity of this matter and the complexities that may arise, such is not surprising. Given the practical nature of this book, I will refer to these controversies in the endnotes rather than in the text. Where such differences of opinion touch upon the practice of discernment, I will discuss them in the text itself.

This book covers the same ground as my earlier book, *Discerning the Will of God: An Ignatian Guide for Christian Decision Making*. It does so, however, with a significant shift of perspective and therefore of content: the former book considered Ignatian discernment of God's will from the perspective of the person discerning; this book from that of the director asked to accompany the discernment. The parallel nature of the two books allows director and directee, if they choose, to employ them simultaneously. Should they do so, the director's task of explaining the material will be greatly simplified.

In my own life, I am deeply grateful to Ignatius for his teaching on discerning God's will. That teaching helps me understand my own vocational discernment and guides me in many choices in life. It provides invaluable guidance when others ask that I accompany their discernment. This teaching is for me a treasure on the spiritual journey. It is my hope that this book will render that treasure more accessible to directors and, through them, to the people they serve.

Text of St. Ignatius

Three Times in Which a Sound and Good Choice May Be Made

The first time is when God our Lord so moves and attracts the will that, without doubting or being able to doubt, the devout soul follows what is shown to it, as St. Paul and St. Matthew did in following Christ our Lord.

The second time is when sufficient clarity and understanding is received through experience of consolations and desolations, and through experience of discernment of different spirits.

The third time is one of tranquility, when one considers first for what purpose man is born—that is, to praise God our Lord and save his soul—and, desiring this, chooses as a means to this end some life or state within the bounds of the Church, so that he may be helped in the service of his Lord and the salvation of his soul. I said a "tranquil time," that is, when the soul is not agitated by different spirits, and uses its natural powers freely and tranquilly.[1]

Chapter One

Beginning the Discernment

They will benefit greatly by entering these exercises with a great heart and with generosity toward their Creator and Lord.

— St. Ignatius of Loyola

In all fruitful discernment, the prime mover is God. Discernment begins, progresses, and concludes with trust in the boundless love of God for both director and discerner. Confidence in that love sustains both along the journey of discernment. It breathes warmth and hope into the process even when clarity may yet appear elusive. Both director and directee know that they have only to do their best, and that God, who seeks us first and desires to be found, will lead them in the process. Gil González Dávila, a Jesuit during Ignatius's lifetime and a key figure in the Ignatian tradition, affirms that one discerning can "trust much in God, who will not let him be deceived; for since he is seeking him with all his heart he will find him. And we can believe nothing else of this divine goodness than that he will welcome whoever so truly seeks him, since he goes out to meet even those who do not seek him."[1]

All that is said in this book is based on trust in that love. It is presumed every step of the way in discernment. That love is our deepest source of confidence as directors that discernment will lead faithfully to God's will.

What Ignatius says of prayer, however, may be said equally of discerning God's will. Prayer is entirely God's *gift*; yet God asks that we *dispose* ourselves to receive that gift. For this reason we give time to prayer, we seek guidance in prayer, and we learn from our tradition how to pray and how to understand what happens when we pray. Such efforts dispose us to receive more richly the gift of prayer.

The same is true of discernment: it is entirely God's gift, but God asks that directors and directees dispose themselves responsibly, in their respective roles, to receive that gift. This book explores the riches of the Ignatian tradition as it prepares directors for this vital task: the responsible guiding of another who seeks to discern God's will.

When a person approaches a director seeking help in such discernment, three factors are involved: the *issue* to be discerned, the *person* discerning, and the *director* who accompanies the discernment. In this chapter, we will discuss each of these as it presents itself in this initial moment. We are asking: What conditions must be present in the issue, the person, and the director for discernment of God's will to begin? We will look to Ignatius for answers.

The Issue

"We love because he first loved us" (1 John 4:19). When human hearts discover that they are loved from all time and infinitely by their God, a yearning to respond awakens. Then human wills thirst for that communion with the divine will that is mutual love—they long to do God's will.[2] They long to live like Jesus, who came into this world to do the will of his Father (Heb. 10:7) and always did what was pleasing to him (John 8:29). This discovery of God's personal love and growth in the desire to respond may take time, in some instances years or decades, and will involve all the complexities of the human heart: its stages of development, experiences in the family, social interactions, and all the joys and wounds that life may bring. Discernment itself of God's will generally requires preparation, and it too will engage the many facets of the human heart. When the desire for discernment arises, however, most fundamentally it does so as a response of love to Love.[3]

Christians seek, then, to discern God's will in the choices they face. At times, the choice is between a good and a bad thing: to be honest or dishonest, to be faithful or unfaithful to marriage vows, priestly ordination, or religious consecration. In such cases, God's will is clear: God never wills what is evil. The options in any choice we discern, Ignatius tells us, must be "lawful within our holy mother the hierarchical Church" (*SpirEx*, 170).[4]

At other times, the choice is between a good thing pertaining to a vocation already chosen and an additional good thing—a mother of three small children, for example, is a talented musician, and her pastor asks if she would lead the parish singing for Holy Week. She will discern God's will by asking whether she can do this additional good thing (leading the singing) compatibly with the good thing God has already asked of her (her vocation as a wife and mother). Likewise the pastor of a busy parish who is asked to lead a two-week pilgrimage to the Holy Land: he too will discern by asking whether this additional good thing (leading the pilgrimage) is compatible with his duties as pastor.

Christians also face many small, daily decisions. A man driving home from work must decide whether to spend time with his son as promised or complete a project at work that suddenly has become urgent. A woman is aware of tension with a friend and must decide whether or not to call her today in the hope of resolving the tension. A man wonders whether a friend who has recently returned to church would welcome an invitation to a prayer meeting or whether it is too soon to suggest this.

In all such decisions, Christians desire that Jesus be Lord (Rom. 10:9). How will they discern in these matters? They will pray, asking the Lord's light. Then they will review the factors involved in the decision: as the man drives home, for example, he will consider how important the time spent with his son is—a birthday celebration, perhaps, or a sports event, or a time of struggle in his son's life—and how urgent the project at work is. They will make their best decision before the Lord and carry it out with peace. Ideally, they will later review their choice and learn from it so that, day by day, Jesus becomes increasingly Lord in all they do.[5]

While Ignatius's teaching on discernment may assist in all the choices thus far described, it applies most directly to a different set of choices. In these choices, both options are *good*, the person is *free* to choose either option, and the choice is *significant* enough to merit a formal process of discernment. Ignatius's teaching on discernment in the *Spiritual Exercises* envisages principally choices such as these.

Primary among them is the choice of one's state of life: marriage, priesthood, or the consecrated life. Choices of career or changes of career may also warrant such discernment. Further choices of this kind may include decisions about new ministries; proposals to one's bishop, religious superior, or boss at work; decisions to relocate with the family; alternatives for the disposal of property; training to be a spiritual director; choices to pursue advanced studies; the decision to adopt a child; and so forth. Always the choice is between good options, always the person is free to choose either, and always the choice is significant. When persons raise choices of this kind with their directors, the issue that calls for Ignatian discernment is present.

In his Spiritual Exercises, Ignatius also applies his process of discernment to a "reform of life" (*SpirEx*, 189). He desires that his "exercises and modes of choosing" (*SpirEx*, 189) assist persons who do not face significant choices but wish to love and serve God more fully in their present circumstances. Such application of Ignatius's teaching on discernment is richly fruitful, and much that we will say in this book will apply to a reform of life as well. Our principal focus, however, will be discernment in significant choices.

The Person

When a person requests help in discerning, a first judgment the director must make is this: Is this person ready to discern? That is, is this person *psychologically* and *spiritually* mature enough for this discernment? Depending on the answer, the process of discernment may or may not be opportune.

If directors do not ask themselves this question, much energy may be expended without result. To enter the process of discernment with persons who are not psychologically and spiritually prepared for it leads to mutual frustration for both the person and the director. After years of engagement with discernment, I believe that this is the major cause of those discernments that continue for years without resolution: the person was not ready for discernment. When directors perceive this to be true, they best help the person by not entering the process of discernment immediately but rather by assisting the person to grow humanly and spiritually as needed, allowing for this growth

all the time necessary. Then, once the person is ready, the discernment will progress with fruit.

First, then, is this person psychologically prepared for discernment?
A young woman, for example, seeks to discern between marriage and
religious life. She approaches a director and asks for help. Directors
in this situation must judge the psychological readiness of this young
woman for such discernment. They will ask themselves, for example:
Is this woman emotionally mature enough for vocational discernment? Is she sufficiently psychologically healthy to discern her calling? Or does she appear anxious, afraid, angry, clinging, distracted,
dependent, or socially inept? Is she mature in her sexuality? Has her
sexual history caused emotional wounds? Have there been addic-
tions in her life? Bouts of depression? Does she struggle with commitments in general? Is she capable of healthy friendships? What clues
to her human readiness for discernment appear in her family history,
her years of study, and her working life? If she does bear emotional
wounds, is she aware of this? Has she sought healing? Is she open to
such healing? How have these wounds affected her image of God,
and what impact does this image have on her ability to trust God and
receive God's love?

If this consideration is always important, it is more so in a culture that in recent decades has increasingly wounded its members.
As divorce, single-parent families, absent fathers, latch-key children,
and similar situations have multiplied, the wounds these inflict have
likewise spread. The absorption in electronic media, promiscuity, and
substance abuse offered to dull the pain only increase the physical and
emotional damage.[6] A first question directors must ask, therefore, is
whether or not the person is psychologically prepared to discern. This
is not to question the person's good will to discern—generally this
will be the case—but whether the person is psychologically mature
enough to discern fruitfully.

If the emotional wounds are significant and if time allows—as in
a vocational discernment, for example, in which a definitive commitment may lie one or more years in the future—directors may wish to
suggest that discerners engage in the counseling process. If so, they
should seek counselors who are both professionally competent and
respectful of the Christian faith. The combination of spiritual growth,

accompanied by spiritual direction, and psychological growth, aided by counseling, powerfully fosters healing and effectively prepares for discernment.

Such judgment regarding psychological readiness for discernment presumes in directors a basic, nonprofessional familiarity with psychology. Directors must be equipped to note significant emotional issues, how these affect directees' relationship with God, and when these may require professional help. The directors' sphere is specifically the spiritual; nonetheless, the greater their psychological awareness, the deeper will be their insight into emotional issues that may affect their directees' discernment.[7]

Directors must also judge the spiritual readiness of the person for discernment. Does this young woman, for example, have a personal relationship with God? What is her image of God? Does it accord with the scriptural revelation of the God who is love? Who is Jesus for her? Does she pray? If so, how? How often? Is her prayer a true encounter with the Lord? Can she sustain times of silence? Is she familiar with Scripture? With the teaching of the Church? Does she live a life of the sacraments? What place does the Eucharist have in her life? How long has she lived as an active member of the Church? Is her life morally in harmony with her desire to discern God's will? Does she sufficiently understand the calling she is considering? Once again, depending on the answers, the director may judge that she is or is not ready for discernment.

If directors perceive that persons are not spiritually prepared to discern, they should not begin the discernment immediately. First they will help these persons grow in their relationship with God, their prayer, and their life in the Church. During this time, directors may also introduce the spiritual tools needed for discernment: meditation and contemplation of Scripture, the first set of rules for discernment, and the examen prayer.[8] Then, when directors see that these persons are spiritually prepared, they will initiate the process of discernment.

Readiness to discern involves more than psychological and spiritual maturity alone: a disposition of heart is also essential, and we will return to this. But without the requisite psychological and spiritual readiness discernment is unlikely to bear fruit. A first service that directors render those who discern is to ensure the presence of this readiness.

The Director

A third consideration regards the directors whom these persons ask to accompany their discernment. From the perspective of directors' preparation to accompany discernment, we may ask: Should they accept this request? What preparation is necessary for them responsibly to agree? This too is a key consideration: a well-prepared director will be of great service to one discerning; another who is unprepared and yet agrees to accompany discernment may contribute to a frustrating process if not to actual harm to the one discerning. The words of Jesuit father Gil González Dávila merit repeating: "Nothing in the whole Exercises is harder than knowing how to manage this matter of discerning God's will properly. Nowhere is more skill or spiritual discretion needed."[9] The same may be said of applying Ignatius's teaching outside the Exercises to assist one discerning. Our question then is this: Assuming preparation for spiritual direction in general—a clear understanding of what spiritual direction is and is not (therapy, pastoral counseling), familiarity with prayer, a basic theological background, the necessary listening and relational skills, and the rest—what specific preparation is necessary for accompanying the discernment of God's will?

The basic elements of this preparation are: knowledge and experience of Ignatian forms of prayer, of the rules for the discernment of spirits, and of the three modes of discerning God's will. We will examine each and discuss how such knowledge and experience are gained in its regard.

This preparation normally is acquired gradually through personal experience, study, and actual direction, ideally with supervision. It is at once demanding and a source of blessing for directors. Those who pursue it not only serve their directees with competence but also grow personally.

Here we can only offer a rapid summary of these Ignatian elements. To describe them in detail would unduly lengthen this book. I have already discussed each in other books to which I refer the reader (see Appendix 4). In this book we will explore one of these elements in detail—Ignatius's three modes of discerning God's will.

I repeat this point because of its importance. From the next chapter to the end of this book, my treatment of our specific topic—the role of the director in the process of discerning God's will—will be complete and detailed. I cannot provide a similar detail with regard to the director's preparation for accompanying this process. As regards the director's specifically Ignatian preparation, I have largely done this in the earlier books mentioned.

The following section of this chapter, therefore, will simply indicate what the director who wishes to apply Ignatius's teaching must know in order to accompany discernment responsibly. To perceive this clearly is already of great value for directors. For some, it will confirm the solidity of their preparation. For others, it will point the way to a more complete preparation and to the fruitfulness that will flow from it.

Ignatian Prayer

At the heart of all discernment is prayer—the human person in relationship with the divine, speaking and listening, sharing and receiving. Discernment is possible only when a person prays faithfully in this fashion.

Directors accompany these persons' prayer and, if necessary, teach them to pray. Directors therefore need to know the forms of Ignatian prayer and to know them not only abstractly but also through personal and ongoing practice.

In Ignatian *meditation*, our reflective capacity is our gateway into the Word of God. If I meditate, for example, on the first beatitude, "Blessed are the poor in spirit, for theirs is the kingdom of heaven" (Matt 5:3),[10] I may ponder why Jesus adds "in spirit" to "poor," and why Jesus says that this disposition gives entry into the kingdom of heaven.[11] As I reflect on this scriptural text, I enter more deeply into its meaning, such that the word speaks to my heart and elicits a response: "Jesus, help me to be poor in spirit. Give me a love for gospel simplicity of life." Through my reflection on his word, God speaks that word to my heart, and my heart speaks to God.[12]

In Ignatian *contemplation*, our imagination is the gateway. If I contemplate, for example, the storm at sea (Matt 8:23–27), I enter the scene imaginatively. I am with the disciples in the boat, sharing in their danger and fear, aware of Jesus asleep, joining in their cry for help. As I live this scene from within, I grasp more deeply the message of this Scripture, and my heart responds: "Jesus, I too can become afraid and feel alone, as though you are asleep. Help me to know that you are close and can calm my storms." Through my imaginative participation in the Gospel event, God speaks his word to my heart and my heart speaks to God.[13]

Preparatory steps precede both methods. Outstanding among them is Ignatius's counsel that I enter the prayer by considering, for the space of an Our Father, the love with which God looks upon me (*SpirEx*, 75).[14] Concluding steps complete the methods, significantly the colloquy, when heart speaks to heart.[15] The director must be familiar with both of these methods and their accompanying steps so as to teach this prayer to the one discerning.

The director must know the Ignatian *review* of prayer (*SpirEx*, 77). When the meditation or contemplation is completed, Ignatius invites the person to review the thoughts and feelings experienced in it.[16] In the review the person asks: As I prayed with the Scripture, what was I thinking? What drew my attention? What struck me? As I prayed with the Scripture, what was I feeling? What stirred in my heart? Did I feel joy? Peace? Anxiety? Did I struggle in any way?[17] This review is critically important in the process of discernment: it supplies the "raw material" on which the discernment will be based. The director must understand this review and be prepared to teach it to the one discerning.

Ignatius further describes a prayer he titles *repetition*.[18] In repetition, we return to our meditation or contemplation and pray again with those points in which we experienced "greater consolation or desolation or greater spiritual appreciation" (*SpirEx*, 62) as we meditated or contemplated. This return disposes us to receive more deeply—greater love, strength, and clarity—in a point already proven fruitful as we prayed.[19] Directors must understand well this form of prayer. When those who discern share their prayer with their directors, these must know when to propose such repetition and for how long.

The young woman discerning between religious life and marriage, for example, imaginatively contemplates the passage of Peter and the catch of fish (Luke 5:1–11). As she hears Jesus ask Peter to "Put out into the deep," she is filled with deep consolation. The director, hearing her describe this experience, will invite her to "repeat" that experience in prayer—to return to it so as to hear more clearly what the Lord is saying through this consolation. Or, as she hears Jesus say to Peter, "Put out into the deep," she may feel deep anxiety and sadness. Here too something important has been touched, and she will need to "repeat" that moment, seeking from the Lord greater clarity and healing.

Repetition is key in discernment. Often it is through repetition that God's leading or the enemy's deceptions become evident. A well-prepared director knows when to suggest such repetition and how to understand what emerges from it.[20]

Finally, directors need familiarity with the *examen* prayer.[21] In this prayer, those discerning look at God's gifts in the day to express gratitude for them, petition God's help to grasp clearly the consolations and desolations of the day or any significant spiritual experience, review that experience, ask forgiveness for any failure to accept God's leading or to reject the enemy's temptations and desolations, and with the Lord plan for the next day.[22] Those discerning who pray the examen gain greater awareness of their spiritual movements and the thoughts arising from them. Such awareness is invaluable for discernment. When those discerning do not know the examen, directors will need to teach it to them and will accompany their experience of it.

Directors, in order to guide discerners in these forms of prayer, must themselves learn them. I believe that we can do this only if we ourselves have ongoing personal experience of praying them. The combination of learning—reading, study, classes—and personal praying of these methods best prepares us to assist others in employing them. Learning these forms of prayer "in the flesh" through clarity of understanding and personal experience is an essential element of preparation for accompanying discernment.

The Discernment of Spirits

In *discernment of God's will*, we seek God's will in specific choices we face. In *discernment of spirits*, we seek to understand the movements of our hearts (consolations and desolations) with their related thoughts (of the good spirit or the enemy) and how we may most fruitfully respond to them.[23] These two forms of discernment are distinct yet overlapping: discernment of spirits is the key element in Ignatius's second mode of discerning God's will, as we will see later in this book. Obviously, then, directors must know well Ignatius's teaching on discernment of spirits.

In his Spiritual Exercises, Ignatius provides two sets of rules for the discernment of spirits (*SpirEx*, 313–36). To accompany one who is discerning God's will requires both theoretical and practical knowledge of these rules. The first set of rules will apply to most who discern; the second set to some.[24] The director must know both sets, when each applies, and how to interpret the discerner's experience in their light. As with Ignatian prayer, this knowledge is the fruit of careful study and personal application of these rules. Competence in applying these rules requires both: not only study but also continued personal exercise of them. We apply these rules personally through our review of prayer, our examen prayer, our retreats, and our own spiritual direction. The more we perceive these rules in our own experience, the better prepared we will be to see them at work in the experience of discerners.

The First Set of Rules

In the title and first four of these rules (*SpirEx*, 313–17), Ignatius lays the foundations for discernment of spirits: the basic paradigm—be aware, understand, take action (title); the ways in which the good spirit and the enemy work corresponding to the essential direction of a person's spiritual life, moving either away from or toward God (rules 1 and 2); and the nature of spiritual consolation and spiritual desolation, the key spiritual movements those discerning must recognize (rules 3 and 4).

In the remaining rules, Ignatius supplies practical tools for rejecting the enemy's desolations and temptations.[25] In rules 5 through 11 (*SpirEx*, 318–24), Ignatius assists those who discern to avoid the trap of spiritual desolation. In times of desolation, Ignatius writes, never change the spiritual proposals you had in place before the desolation began (rule 5); strive rather to reject the desolation itself through increased prayer, meditation, examination, and suitable penance (rule 6); ponder the truths that will sustain you in desolation—that God's grace is always sufficient to resist it without harm (rule 7); strive to be patient, to stay the course, reflecting that desolation always passes and that consolation will return (rule 8); explore the reasons why a God who loves you permits you to experience this desolation, that is, consider the growth God desires to give you through resisting this desolation (rule 9); prepare for future desolation in time of consolation (rule 10); remain humble in consolation and trusting in desolation (rule 11).

The final three rules (*SpirEx*, 325–27) discuss the enemy's temptations and how to avoid them. Ignatius counsels those discerning to reject these temptations in their very beginning and before they can "snowball" (rule 12); to refuse the enemy's urgings to keep his disheartening insinuations secret from their directors and to share these openly with them (rule 13); to identify well their weakest point, that aspect of their spiritual lives in which they are most exposed to the enemy's traps, and to work to strengthen this point (rule 14).

These fourteen rules are critically important for those who discern. Directors must be able to teach these rules and to help those who discern to apply them. Once the rules are learned, discerners perceive how ably Ignatius equips them to reject the enemy's desolations and temptations. When directors understand these rules well and share them opportunely, those discerning are set free to progress in their discernment.

The Second Set of Rules

A first tactic of the enemy, then, is the attempt to discourage through desolation and "manifest deceits" (*SpirEx*, 326). Those who begin to dedicate themselves to God with new energy may experience temptations like these: If I say yes to the Lord's call, it will be unbearably heavy; I will be criticized by others; I will lose the respect of family members and friends, and so forth (*SpirEx*, 9). Those who discern and who are troubled by the enemy's desolations and more evident temptations need the wisdom of the first set of rules.

Others who discern may have advanced further on the spiritual journey and dedicate themselves wholeheartedly to love and serve God. With such generous persons, Ignatius says, the enemy may adopt a new tactic: rather than attempt to discourage through spiritual desolation and obvious temptation (first set of rules), he may now disguise himself as an angel of light (*SpirEx*, 332) and bring spiritual consolation with an attraction toward a good choice, but a good choice different from that which God desires (second set of rules). An example will illustrate this point.

A dedicated pastor, a man of deep prayer and a faithful priest, approaches his spiritual director for help in discernment.[26] His bishop had asked him three years earlier to be pastor of a parish riddled by scandal and division. He had said yes, and his efforts slowly have borne fruit, not only fostering healing but also awakening new energy in the parish. Numbers are rising, the school is stronger, the liturgy is alive, and spiritual and service-oriented initiatives in the parish are growing.

One day the pastor prays with the beatitudes in the Gospel of Luke (6:20–26). His heart is pierced by the first of these, "Blessed are you poor, for yours is the kingdom of God."[27] He is struck by Jesus' deep love for the poor and the marginalized. A great joy and closeness to God awakens in his heart with a strong attraction to leave the comfort of the suburban parish and serve the poor more directly in an inner-city parish. He now wonders: Is the joy I am experiencing an indication that God wills that I approach the bishop and request a transfer to the inner-city parish? How will he discern? And how will his director assist him in this discernment?

In this scenario, the pastor does not experience spiritual desolation, nor is he tempted in any obvious way as, for example, by discouragement in his priestly service. The first set of rules, therefore, will not help this pastor.

The question he must answer is this: Is that joy and closeness to God—that spiritual consolation—of the good spirit and therefore a sign that God wants him to request a transfer to an inner-city parish? Or is it the enemy, disguised as an angel of light, bringing spiritual consolation with an attraction for a good and holy thing—direct service of the materially poor in imitation of Jesus—that will undermine the rich fruit of the pastor's present service and therefore ultimately lead to diminishment in the Church? How can directors help this pastor and all dedicated laypersons, religious, and priests who, in their respective states of life, may face such refined discernment?

To assist directors, Ignatius supplies his second set of rules (*SpirEx*,

328–36). After the introductory material (title, rule 1), Ignatius describes a form of spiritual consolation that only God can give: consolation without a preceding cause—that is, without a stirring of the heart or a specific thought from which the consolation arose (rule 2). Consolation without a preceding cause is only of God and, when identified as such, may be trusted implicitly.[28] Directors must be able to recognize such consolation should God give this grace to those who discern.

Ignatius next addresses the more common case of spiritual consolation with a preceding cause—that is, a consolation that arises from a stirring of the heart or a thought that precedes and gives rise to the consolation (rules 3 to 7). Thus, for example, the consolation that the pastor experiences in praying with the first beatitude: his thoughts about these words of Jesus precede and occasion the consolation that follows. When, Ignatius says, the consolation arises from a preceding cause, it may be either of the good spirit or of the enemy. Discernment is necessary, and clearly much depends on this discernment. The pastor's discernment, for example, will affect the spiritual lives of hundreds of persons.

In this case, Ignatius asks directors to guide those discerning to note the *beginning, middle,* and *end* of the thoughts arising from this consolation. For the pastor, this is the thought of asking the bishop for a transfer to an inner-city parish. Whether the consolation is of the good or the bad spirit, the beginning—the initial thoughts—will be holy and good. At this initial point, if the enemy is imitating the good spirit he will bring only what is good and holy. If these thoughts are indeed of the good spirit, they will remain fully good and holy as they unfold (the middle) and in the conclusion to which they lead (the end). If they are of the enemy, the middle will already reveal a diminishment of goodness and holiness, a diminishment even more evident in the end to which they lead.

If, for example, the pastor's thoughts of asking the bishop for an inner-city parish are of the good spirit, as the thoughts progress over the months (middle) no diminishment will occur in the fervor of the priest's spiritual life: his love of God, his interior peace, and his confidence in God will remain as rich as they were before this thought arose. Likewise, when the thoughts are fully formulated and the pastor feels ready to speak with the bishop (end), the proposed project as it then appears will reveal no diminishment with respect to his present ministry, no sign that the new ministry will lead to less good in the Church than his present service. Evidently, he will need the wise accompaniment of a prepared director to discern this.

If, on the other hand, the spiritual consolation and thoughts are of the enemy, a diminishment will occur either in the priest's own spiritual life, or in the fruitfulness of the final project by contrast with his present ministry, or both of these. Such diminishment, Ignatius says, is a clear sign of the enemy: in this case, it would reveal that the spiritual consolation the pastor felt in praying with the beatitudes and the thought of the inner-city parish were of the enemy from the beginning. The director's task in such cases is to help the person note the progression of the thoughts and verify whether or not this diminishment occurs.

Finally, Ignatius indicates that although consolation without preceding cause is always of God, and that the proposals that arise *during* it may be followed without hesitation, the same is not true of proposals that arise *after* the consolation has passed, when the person remains warmed by it (rule 8).[29] These latter proposals may be of the good spirit, but may also arise from the enemy or from the person who experienced this consolation. They must, therefore, be carefully discerned before they are pursued.

A dedicated woman, for example, has long felt an attraction toward serving as a spiritual director. Others seek her spiritual help, and her pastor has encouraged her to consider this. She makes a retreat to seek the Lord's will in this matter. One morning, she enters the chapel, sits, and suddenly is filled with a powerful sense of God's deep love for her. Her heart is profoundly moved, and her tears express her joy. She knows that this experience is pure gift, and her heart overflows with gratitude to know herself so utterly loved. The next days of the retreat continue to be filled with the warmth of that blessed experience in the chapel.

As the retreat continues, the woman reflects on that experience. She perceives that something new has entered her relationship with God through it. She also senses that this new manifestation of God's love is an invitation to show her love too in a new way. It seems evident that this new way is the service of spiritual direction. With joy in her heart, the woman concludes that her discernment is complete: God's will is that she serve as spiritual director.[30]

Has she discerned well? Has she rightly understood God's call? In Ignatius's terms, her conclusion is a proposal made *after* the consolation without preceding cause, while she still remains warmed by it. Before she acts on this conclusion, therefore, her director must help her discern carefully whether this conclusion truly is of God. The director will recognize that the experience in the chapel was most likely a consolation without preceding cause, and therefore surely of God. The woman's conclusion, however, that this experience revealed God's will regarding spiritual direction was reached not *in* the experience but only days *after,* while she remained warmed by the experience. The director will explain Ignatius's guideline to her and accompany her as her discernment continues.

We have provided here only a rapid overview of these two sets of rules. As is evident, directors must learn them well and be prepared to apply them when discerners share their experiences.

The Three Modes of Discerning God's Will

These modes are the centerpiece of all the director must know to accompany Ignatian discernment. Ignatius learned from experience that God may reveal his will in one or more of three modes: through a clarity that the person simply cannot doubt (first mode), through discernment of spirits (second mode), or through a preponderance of reasons for God's greater glory (third mode).[31] Directors must assimilate them well in theory and practice. Because we will examine these in detail later,[32] little need be said here beyond noting the importance of this proficiency. Learning these three modes and how to apply them is the heart of the "skill and spiritual discernment" required for accompanying discernment of God's will.[33]

A Process of Preparation

Ignatian forms of prayer, the rules for the discernment of spirits, the three modes of discerning God's will: these are the tools directors need to accompany discernment responsibly and well. How can we gain this preparation?

The best way to learn these Ignatian tools is by making the Spiritual Exercises. In the Exercises we experience them in their original setting, and we assimilate them through practicing them with guidance. The full Ignatian retreat, where possible, is the ideal. This may be done as thirty days in a retreat house or in daily life over several months. Directors who make this experience will find that it will bless greatly all future spiritual direction. Eight-day Ignatian retreats, made once or more often, are also valuable means toward learning these tools. Having experienced them in the Exercises, we will see more clearly how to employ them when discernment takes place in daily life.

The study of which we have spoken is most fruitful when it follows the retreat. Such study allows us to penetrate more deeply the teaching we have already experienced. When reading and classes illuminate experience, that learning is most effective.[34] Experience is invaluable, but directors need more than experience if they are to guide others. They must find ways of studying Ignatius's teaching on discerning God's will.

Directors themselves need accompaniment in this preparation. Those who offer spiritual direction should themselves receive spiritual direction. They may also choose a mentor, a director experienced in Ignatian discernment, to whom they can turn as they grow in accompanying discernment. Finally and more broadly, supervision in our service of spiritual direction is highly beneficial.[35]

In this chapter we have explored the elements necessary for discernment to begin. We are now ready to approach discernment itself.

Chapter Two

Laying the Foundation

Our one desire and choice should be what better leads us to the end for which we are created.

—St. Ignatius of Loyola

A solid foundation permits the construction of a solid edifice. The same is true, Ignatius writes, of every well-made discernment. He describes this beginning point as the "foundation" on which the discernment is built and the first "principle" from which all else follows in the discernment (*SpirEx*, 23). Gil González Dávila terms this "the foundation of the spiritual structure" in the discernment,[1] and Juan Alfonso de Polanco adds that "the entire moral structure [of the discernment] is built upon it."[2] The Official Directory asserts of the one discerning that "the deeper he lays this foundation the firmer will be his edifice" of discernment.[3]

Ignatius supplies this foundation at the beginning of his Spiritual Exercises (*SpirEx*, 23) and returns to it repeatedly throughout the discernment.[4] In it, he clarifies for the one discerning the end toward which every "healthy and good" (*SpirEx*, 175) discernment is a means. A look at his own words will illustrate his meaning.

The Texts

The primary text Ignatius titles the "Principle and Foundation" (*SpirEx*, 23), a passage that directors must know well and know how to present to discerners. Ignatius desires that this be done when giving the Spiritual Exercises; in significant discernments outside the Exercises as well, directors will generally find that the discernment proceeds more solidly when they present this foundation from the outset.[5] Below in this chapter, we will explore ways in which they might do this.

Ignatius begins by painting the large picture: "Man is created to praise, reverence, and serve God our Lord, and by this means to save his soul."[6] This is the starting point of all discernment: the love with which the Creator has given us life, the call to respond to that love in service of the One who loves us, and by this means, when our lives here on earth have ended, to enter eternal blessedness with God.

An important consequence follows: "The other things on the face of the earth are created for man to help him attain the end for which he is created." Discerners are to see "the other things on the face of the earth"—that is, the places where they live, the occupations they have or may have, their relationships, and so forth—in their true light as means given by God toward the end just described: to praise, reverence, and serve God our Lord and so gain the joy of eternal communion with God. They must view the many created realities that affect their lives in this light if they are to discern well.

Ignatius's text continues: "Consequently, man must use them inasmuch as they help him toward his end, and must rid himself of them inasmuch as they hinder him." This truth will be a sure guide when discerners struggle between contrasting attractions and resistances in regard to the "things on the face of the earth."

Such considerations lead to the key disposition required for good discernment. This disposition is, Ignatius says, "that you place yourself totally in his [God's] hands, since this is the foundation for finding what we desire," that is, God's will in the present discernment.[7] We must, Ignatius elaborates, "make ourselves indifferent [*indiferentes*, that is, available, free, not bound to one option in the choice, open to wherever God will lead in the discernment] with regard to all created things in all that is allowed to the choice of our free will and not prohibited to it" (*SpirEx*, 23). A married woman, for example, or a parish priest cannot be open (*indiferente*) to fulfilling or not fulfilling the commitments of their callings—the married woman to love and care for her children, and the priest to provide the sacraments for his parishioners. These tasks are clearly God's will for them.[8] If, however, they are discerning God's will in a choice regarding which they are free—the married woman may consider a change of job or the priest a new initiative in the parish—then, Ignatius says, to discern well they must place themselves totally in God's hands, open and available to whichever alternative God will show to be his will.

Ignatius concretizes this disposition through examples: "such that for our part we do not desire health more than illness, riches more than poverty, to be held in honor or dishonor, a long life more than a short life, and so with all the rest." The conclusion follows: "Our one desire and choice should be what better leads us to the end for which we are created." Ignatius asks discerners to reflect repeatedly on these foundational truths before they undertake discernment. If they do, their discernment will be built on the truths that alone permit authentic Christian discernment.

Once discerners have entered the discernment, each time they pray Ignatius urges them to begin by asking for this disposition. The preparatory prayer is, he says, "to ask grace of God our Lord that all my intentions, actions, and operations be purely directed to the service and praise of his Divine Majesty" (*SpirEx*, 46). As they pray during the weeks or months of their discernment, discerners thus ask daily for the disposition described in the Principle and Foundation: that everything in their lives—their intentions, actions, and operations— be solely directed to God's service and praise. As this grace deepens in them, discerners grow in readiness to discern. Directors may consider inviting discerners to make this prayer daily when discerning outside the retreat, in ordinary life.

On the threshold of discernment, Ignatius reminds them once again: "In every good choice, as far as depends on us, the eye of our intention must be simple, looking only at why I am created, that is, for the praise of God our Lord and the salvation of my soul" (*SpirEx*, 169). In the discernment itself, Ignatius repeats this theme: "One considers first for what purpose man is born, that is, to praise God our Lord and save his soul" (*SpirEx*, 177). And yet again: "It is necessary to keep as my aim the end for which I am created, that is, to praise God our Lord and save my soul" (*SpirEx*, 179). Ignatius intends that these foundational truths permeate the entire process of discernment. Directors will find ways to help discerners keep them alive in their consciousness as they discern.

The Foundation Today

In past years, I assumed that I need not say much to those discerning about this foundation. These were generous, dedicated, faith-filled people who loved the Lord. I thought the foundation—that we are created to praise, reverence, and serve God our Lord and by this means to enter eternal life—could be taken almost for granted in such persons, and that little emphasis on it was necessary.

More recently I have come to believe the contrary: that Ignatius's foundation is more important than ever, and that explicit focus on it is necessary for discerners today. In sixteenth-century Europe, Ignatius asked even the most generous of his retreatants—future saints like Pierre Favre, Francis Xavier, and others—to consider the foundation before entering discernment. In our highly secularized culture today, this consideration is even more vital.

Ignatius's Principle and Foundation is completely absent in contemporary culture: in mainstream television, digital content, academic circles, newspapers, popular journals, literature, scholarly writing, psychological circles, and so forth, discerners are unlikely to encounter these truths. Most often they have received a contrasting vision of life: with many nuances, the basic message is the same—persons create their own meaning in life. Slogans abound: "It's my life"; "I want what feels right for me"; "Follow your bliss"; "Just do it"; "I want to be fulfilled"; "It's my choice"; and the like. These approaches contain mixtures of truth and error, but are completely inadequate for discernment of God's will.

Even the most dedicated persons, therefore, will benefit from Ignatius's invitation to reflect on the Principle and Foundation before they discern. Unless *this* foundation is established, authentic discernment is not possible. Its absence explains many processes of discernment that languish and never lead to clarity. Its presence forms a solid basis for fruitful discernment. For those who have already assimilated the foundation, a refreshment will be sufficient. For others, more time, reflection, and prayer will be necessary as they absorb the foundation consciously and explicitly, perhaps for the first time. This will be one—and not the least—blessing their process of discernment will offer them.

In some settings, the Principle and Foundation is presented as immersion in God's love for us. The most foundational truth is indeed that God, who is love, loves me personally, deeply, and eternally. Presented in this light, persons pray with scriptural texts that speak of this love: Isaiah 43:1–7; Psalm 139:1–18; Romans 8:26–39, and similar texts. Below I will supply a list of such texts. Directors who present the foundation in this light know how fruitful it can be: persons who have long doubted God's love for them begin to realize how that love embraces them. As they pray, they find new hope and courage.

This presentation of the Principle and Foundation, for all its richness, is insufficient for Ignatius's purpose in discerning God's will. The Principle and Foundation presents a set of truths—all of them suffused with God's personal love—regarding our creation, our end, and other created things as means to that end, concerning which discerners need clarity, and which leads to a disposition of heart: "Our one desire and choice should be that which better leads us to the end for which we are created." When these truths are clear and fresh in discerners' minds and this disposition takes root in their hearts, the Principle and Foundation has achieved its purpose. Directors who accompany those discerning will need to present it this way, in its fullness.

Presenting the Foundation

Ignatius's Text

How directors present the foundation may vary depending on the background of those they accompany. Directors will find that some discerners benefit from reflecting on Ignatius's text as he wrote it (*SpirEx*, 23). Having explained Ignatius's words, directors may invite them to read, reread, and reflect frequently on Ignatius's words for several days or weeks, as time allows. Ignatius's words are succinct, clear, and effective in presenting the foundation.

Some discerners will benefit from using Ignatius's words just as he wrote them. Others may find a contemporary rendering of the text easier to assimilate. In the first appendix, I include both the original and my contemporary rendering.

Juan Alfonso de Polanco, in a classic and widely used outline, summarizes the Principle and Foundation according to the four points that discerners are to assimilate. First, that "We are created for this end, that we might praise and reverence our God, and by serving him be saved." Second, that "The other things were created on earth for our sake, to help us to the aforesaid end." Third, that "From this it follows that creatures are to be used or abstained from insofar as they help or hinder us toward our end." And fourth, that "As far as we are able, we ought to be indifferent [available, ready to choose whatever God will show to be his will] toward all created things, and not seek health more than sickness, riches more than poverty, honor more than contempt, a long life more than a short one." Rather, Polanco concludes, "Instead of all these things we ought to desire those more that lead us more to our end."[9] When directors see that discerners have sufficiently understood and embraced these four points, they know these persons are ready for the next step in discernment. If discerners have not grasped and espoused these truths, directors should invite them to continue praying and reflecting on them until the foundation takes root in them.

Scriptural Texts

Those discerning will benefit from praying with biblical texts that express the truths of the foundation. Such prayer is an effective way to assimilate these truths and to seek from the Lord a heart that loves them. This biblically based presentation of the foundation may be made alone or together with reflection on Ignatius's text as described above. Directors will choose the specific approach according to what will best serve individual discerners.

I supply here a selection of scriptural texts that I have used over the years.[10] I offer them as suggestions, indicative of texts that help embrace the foundation. They may be prayed in an Ignatian retreat or in daily life when discernment occurs in that context. Directors may change or add to these as they judge helpful for discerners.

God's Love

These first texts express the foundational truth of God's love for those discerning. Some already live in this truth, and prayer with these texts will refresh a habitual awareness. For these, a conscious dwelling on this truth, even if briefly, will help to begin discernment well.

Others may struggle more to believe that God loves them. When family life and subsequent experiences have not shown them that they are lovable, the leap to accepting God's love for them may be great. In our culture, such situations are all too common. Directors may need to prolong these discerners' prayer with texts that reveal God's love for them. In this case, more texts than those given here may be necessary. Those provided will suggest further texts that serve to seek this grace.

As discerners pray with these texts, directors should watch to note those that particularly touch the discerners' hearts. Directors should then invite the discerners to pray further with these texts—the Ignatian prayer of repetition described above. If God reveals his love in a particular way through a certain text, directors should invite discerners to pray with that text as long as God continues to give grace through it (*SpirEx*, 76). This principle—to continue to pray with a text as long as God gives grace through it—will hold for all prayer with Scripture throughout the process of discernment. If directors apply this principle, they will greatly assist discerners to grasp God's leading in the process.

The following texts may be prayed in the order given or in the order that directors judge best suited to individual discerners:

Matthew 11:25–30	Come to me all you who are burdened, and I will give you rest.[11]
Isaiah 55:1–13	Let everyone who thirsts come to the waters.
Jeremiah 29:11–14	I will give you a future and a hope.
Isaiah 43:1–7	You are precious in my eyes, and honored, and I love you.
Psalm 139:1–18	God's love at the source of my being; God's closeness to me.
Romans 8:31–39	Nothing can separate us from the love of God.
1 John 4:7–19	Love casts out fear.
Psalm 27	The Lord is my salvation; I need not fear.
Galatians 2:19–21	The Son of God loved me.
Romans 5:6–11	God showed his love for us.

Isaiah 49:13–16	I will not forget you.
Isaiah 54:1–10	I love you with everlasting love.
Isaiah 62:1–5	The Lord delights in you.
Hosea 11:1–11	My compassion for my people grows warm within me.
Ezekiel 34:11–16	I myself will shepherd my sheep.
Ephesians 1:3–10	Blessed with every spiritual blessing.

Availability to God in the Discernment

Availability to God is the key disposition for discernment, and Ignatius presents it from the start in his Principle and Foundation. The texts that follow invite discerners to pray for this disposition as they approach discernment. Discerners need not possess this disposition totally at this point; later in the process, as we will see, this will be essential. What is necessary to begin discernment is that discerners understand, desire, and seek this disposition in prayer. Should directors note strong resistance to this availability—the readiness to accept either alternative should God reveal it to be his will—they will need to see at least a sincere desire to seek it before proceeding further. Such desire gives founded hope that as these persons continue in the process, they will receive the grace of this availability.

The following texts may help discerners seek this grace. These texts may be prayed in the order and number that directors judge best for each discerner. Similar texts may be added if needed. Here too, directors will encourage discerners to pray unhurriedly with texts that especially open their hearts to this availability.

Jeremiah 18:1–6	Like clay in the potter's hand.
Isaiah 6:1–8	Here I am; send me.
Philippians 3:1–11	I have given all things for the sake of Christ.
Genesis 22:1–18	Readiness to give all God asks.
Luke 14:25–35	Complete availability: the condition of discipleship.
Psalm 40	To do your will is my delight.
Luke 1:26–38	Let it be done to me according to your word.
Genesis 12:1–9	Abraham leaves all to follow God's leading.
Mark 10:17–31	Leaving all when Jesus asks.

Luke 9:57–62   Following Jesus without conditions.
Matthew 26:36–46   Not my will but yours be done.
1 Samuel 3:1–10   Speak, Lord, your servant is listening.
Matthew 13:44–45   Giving all for the Kingdom.
Matthew 6:25–33   Seek first the Kingdom.
John 3:22–30   He must increase, but I must decrease.

As discerners reflect prayerfully on Ignatius's text (*SpirEx*, 23) and pray with scriptural passages of this kind, their readiness or lack of readiness for discernment will emerge. When directors judge that discerners are sufficiently rooted in the foundation, and are available to God or at least sincerely desirous of growing in this availability, they will invite them to the next stage in discernment: the removal, with God's grace, of interior obstacles to discernment.

Chapter Three

Removing the Obstacles

The eye of our intention must be simple.
                                        —St. Ignatius of Loyola

Once the foundation is laid, the next step is to remove the obstacles. From the outset in his Spiritual Exercises, Ignatius addresses this need. These Exercises comprise, he tells us, "every manner of preparing and disposing the soul to rid itself of all disordered affections, and once these are removed, to seek and find the divine will" (*SpirEx*, 1). Before discerners may profitably seek God's will, they must prepare by pursuing freedom from "disordered affections."

Later in the text, Ignatius summarizes his retreat as "Spiritual Exercises for conquering oneself and ordering one's life, without choosing under the influence of any disordered affection" (*SpirEx*, 21). When he describes the discernment itself, Ignatius repeatedly renews this emphasis: the choice must not be made out of disordered affections (*SpirEx*, 169, 172, 179).

What are these disordered affections? They are any attachment of the heart not "purely and properly for the love of God" (*SpirEx*, 150) and not in harmony with the order established in the foundation: that we are created out of love to praise and serve God in this life and so enter eternal blessedness; and that, therefore, all places, relationships, possessions, and occupations are to be chosen inasmuch as they better help us to serve God and gain eternal life. These disordered affections include anything sinful or even, without being sinful, simply apart from a God-centered love: not "purely and properly for the love of God." The removal of such disordered affections frees the heart to say "yes" to whatever God will show to be his will.

Thus a man may wish to discern God's will regarding a career in medicine or finance. As he approaches this discernment, his heart may be set on medicine because he desires the prestige this profession normally signifies. He may desire this simply for self-aggrandizement; he may also, more or less consciously, desire it because he was marginalized in his family and hopes in this way to win its respect. A woman who genuinely loves the Lord may incline toward the cloistered life in part from fear of human relationships. A young man who feels the call to priesthood may resist because he will lose the esteem of his peers. A young woman whose parents divorced, knowing that a young man will propose marriage, may fear the commitment marriage implies.

As is evident, such attractions and resistances not "purely and properly for the love of God" may touch deep places in the human heart. With sensitivity and reverence, directors will need to assist discerners to find freedom from them.[1] Obviously, unless this freedom is present, God's will cannot be discerned. A failure to recognize and address such attachments before entering the discernment proper will impair the entire process.

The need for freedom from sinful attachments is clear, though this may require courage on the part of discerners. Ignatius explicitly invites discerners to seek this freedom in the first week of his Exercises (*SpirEx*, 24–72), and this need applies equally to discernment outside the retreat. The experience of one young man who prayed for this freedom may stand for many. In it, both the courage required and the fruitfulness of this prayer are evident. Such experiences reveal why directors must not fear to invite discerners, with love and sensitivity, into a prayer that fosters the freedom to discern. Recalling his discernment, this man writes:

> The first week of the *Spiritual Exercises* focuses on the need for the sinner to approach Jesus Christ with a thoroughly honest examination of life. . . . I dreaded to admit my responsibility, fearing God's rejection of me. However, because St. Ignatius instructed retreatants to take their sinfulness to Jesus Christ on the cross, I learned that he died precisely to forgive these sins.

What amazed me was that the more honest I could be
before our Lord in confessing my sins, the greater peace I felt.
No longer was "Jesus loves sinners" simply words. This was a
powerful experience. . . .

Knowing myself as a sinner who is loved to the death by
Jesus Christ gave me a freedom to offer myself to be whatever the Lord wanted me to be. The specific vocation—Jesuit
priest or brother, diocesan priest, husband and father of a
family, or single layman—no longer mattered because I knew
that Christ loved me so much that *anything* He wanted for me
would be the best thing for me.[2]

Knowing himself as "a sinner who is loved to the death by Jesus
Christ" sets this man free to discern, as his final words powerfully
indicate. At this point, the obstacles have been removed, and the road
to discernment is open.

The key focus in this prayer, as the account also indicates, is the
infinite love of Jesus. Standing before the cross of Christ, whose love
leads him to accept death for us, discerners learn how deeply "we
are loved and held by God in all our brokenness and littleness."[3] The
entire movement of this stage of preparation consists in bringing "our
brokenness and littleness" to the love and mercy of Jesus (*SpirEx*, 53,
61, 71). Directors must present this stage in that light if it is to be healing and to prepare discernment.

Directors will also need to accompany this stage with sensitivity
to individual discerners. Some, well rooted in God's love and blessed
with robust psychological strength, will seek this purification without
significant anxiety, as in the account just given. The quest for this freedom always requires courage, but for these the necessary spiritual and
psychological conditions are present, and the process will be fruitful.

Others, less formed spiritually and more wounded psychologically,
may struggle more as they seek purification from sinfulness.[4] Directors may even wonder whether it is wise to invite them to pray for this
purification. In fact, unless presented with care, this step may cause
them tension and pain. But such prayer for purification should never
be omitted—even the holiest must ask God's forgiveness daily, and
growing freedom from sinfulness prepares a well-made discernment.

For such discerners, however, I believe it wisest not to attempt Ignatius's direct approach to prayer for this purification: review of sin in salvation history, of sin in my own life, and of eternal punishment for unrepented serious sin (*SpirEx*, 45–71). A gentler approach to this same issue will allow these discerners to profit in the measure of their readiness. In this approach, the same truths are presented but less directly and through scriptural texts that emphasize God's mercy toward sincere but struggling human hearts. Examples include Jesus' encounter with Zacchaeus (Luke 19:1–10), the healing of the paralytic (Mark 2:1–12), the parables of mercy in Luke 15, and many similar texts. Throughout, the same call to purification is present, but in a way these discerners can absorb. This approach will not cause them anxiety and will lead them toward purification. I will indicate below a number of scriptural texts suited to this approach.

Freedom for discernment may also be necessary on the psychological level. Years of experience convince me that "attachments" arising from psychological wounds abound today, above all in the younger generations, and directors must note these when they are present. At times, counseling and medication may be indicated. If the wounds are deep, directors may need to suggest a time of healing before entering discernment. This time is not lost: such healing will not only prepare discernment but will bless the discerners' entire spiritual journey.

The Process

At this point in the process, discerners must be praying daily. If their occupations permit, attending Mass during the week will richly dispose them to receive grace. Should they not know how to meditate (reflective approach) or contemplate (imaginative approach), directors must teach them these methods.[5] Instruction in the preparatory steps (review of the scriptural text, composition, asking for the grace desired) and concluding steps (above all, the colloquy) will assist them to enter and end the prayer with fruit.[6] Directors will supply biblical texts for prayer suited to the grace sought at this stage. A list of such texts is provided below.

How much time should discerners dedicate to this daily prayer with Scripture? In his retreat, Ignatius asks for an hour with each text. If discerners have or can acquire the habit of praying for an hour, and if they have the time compatibly with their other responsibilities, this practice will serve the discernment well. Discerners who at this stage would find an hour daunting or who do not have the time may pray for a shorter time. Less than thirty minutes, however, is no longer ideal since, in our age that "lives too fast" (Thoreau), quieting the heart and entering the Word generally require at least this much time.[7] If less than thirty minutes is all that is possible, then we must trust that God will not refuse grace to those who do their best. But without this prayer, discernment, as Ignatius conceives it, is not possible.

Directors should now teach discerners how to review their prayer (*SpirEx*, 77).[8] They will invite discerners to review their prayer with Scripture each day, noting their thoughts and feelings and anything significant that occurred as they prayed. Directors will also encourage them to record in their journals what emerges from this review. These reviews and this journaling provide discerners with a clear awareness of their spiritual experience and best prepare them to share that experience with their directors.

At this point directors should also introduce the examen prayer. As they pray the examen, discerners will increasingly find God in their experience and uncover the deceptions of the enemy throughout the day. They will learn that discernment incorporates not only the formal times of prayer, but also the entire day. They will grow in the ability to recognize times of spiritual consolation and desolation, and to notice the thoughts, attractions, and resistances they experience. Directors will need to guide discerners gradually into this prayer, explaining it and encouraging them as they pray it daily.[9] The examen made well permits discerners to grasp further indications of God's will and greatly strengthens the process.

Discerners should meet with their directors monthly, if possible. Later, as they enter the discernment proper, directors and discerners may wish to meet more often. Directors should also help discerners understand the purpose of this meeting: to share their spiritual experience since the last meeting. For this purpose, their journals with their daily recording of prayer with Scripture and the examen will be invaluable instruments. Directors will invite discerners to share what God has done and also any tactics of the enemy they may have experienced. They will encourage discerners to describe their spiritual consolations and desolations, with any related attractions, resistances, and thoughts. Directors will help discerners understand the experience they share: how God is speaking to them through it and which traps of the enemy to avoid. Directors will note whether the grace sought—here that of freedom from "disordered affections"—has been given and when discerners may be ready for the next stage in discernment.

At this point, directors may propose the sacrament of reconciliation to discerners. Ignatius considers this sacrament a valuable resource for the purification that prepares discernment, and the experience of many confirms his view.[10] He counsels that the confessor be someone other than the director.[11]

Regular confession during this time may assist the process. Depending on discerners' formation and practice of this sacrament—for some it may be new—directors may need to explain the sacrament and the grace it offers. Some discerners may benefit from the general confession Ignatius proposes in the Spiritual Exercises (*SpirEx*, 44). Directors will assist them as necessary to decide with respect to this option.

As this outline of the process indicates, the growth this stage of discernment alone offers discerners is significant. Lived well, this stage brings healing and offers rich formation in the spiritual life.

Scriptural Texts

As in the preceding chapter, I provide a selection of scriptural texts suited for prayer at this point in the process. As before, directors may use or modify them according to the discerners' need. Directors who adopt the gentler approach described may choose to omit some of these: a review of the texts and knowledge of the discerner will guide their selection.[12] This list adheres, with some freedom, to the order of Ignatius's five exercises of prayer in Week One of the Spiritual Exercises (*SpirEx*, 45–71). Directors will note experiences of relevance as discerners pray with these texts and will invite the discerners to return to them for further prayer.

| Genesis 3:1–24 | Sin and its consequences; the hope of redemption. |
| Romans 5:12–21 | Through one man came sin; through one man came life. |

Romans 7:14–25	Who will deliver me? Thanks be to God through Jesus Christ.
1 John 1:5–2:6	If we confess our sins, he will cleanse us.
Romans 5:6–11	While we were yet sinners, Christ died for us.
John 8:1–11	Neither do I condemn you.
Mark 2:1–12	"My son, your sins are forgiven."
Luke 7:36–50	Her sins are forgiven, for she loved much.
Luke 18:9–14	God, be merciful to me.
Luke 19:1–10	"He also is a son of Abraham."
1 Cor 13:1–7	A look at my life in the light of love: Is my love like this?
Romans 12:1–21	A program of Christian life: Do I live like this?
Ephesian 4:1–32	A life worthy of our calling: Do I live this calling?
Psalm 51	Wash me, and I will be whiter than snow.
Matthew 25:31–46	What matters most in life and shapes our eternal destiny.
Luke 16:19–31	This life and the next.
Psalm 130	With the Lord is plenteous redemption.
Luke 15	Parables of mercy: the lost sheep, the lost coin, the prodigal son.
Hebrews 4:14–16	Let us draw near with confidence.
Psalm 136	Give thanks to the Lord, for his love is everlasting.
Psalm 103	As far as the east is from the west, so far does God remove our transgressions.
Isaiah 54:1–10	With everlasting love I will have compassion on you.

When directors judge that the grace of purification has been sufficiently granted,[13] they will invite discerners to enter the next stage in the process. Building on the earlier stages, Ignatius now asks discerners to seek the disposition of heart that alone permits true discernment.

Chapter Four

Forming the Disposition

I should be like a balance at equilibrium, ready to follow
whatever I perceive to be more for the glory and praise of
God our Lord and the salvation of my soul.

—St. Ignatius of Loyola

Regarding the interior disposition necessary for discerning God's
will, Casanovas writes, "The existence of this precious disposition
or its absence principally determines whether the discernment will be
made well or poorly."[1] *Principally determines*: we touch here the core
of that which permits right discernment. At this point in the process,
the foundation is established and the obstacles are being removed.
The final preparation consists in the consolidation of this disposition
through prayer with Christ in the Gospels. Ignatius cannot insist on
this disposition too much; as Casanovas affirms, whether the discernment will be made well or poorly depends primarily upon its presence
or absence.

A key role, therefore, of directors is to ensure that discerners possess this disposition before admitting them to the discernment proper.
As they accompany their directees toward discernment, directors
must ask themselves: Am I aware of the importance of this disposition? Do I know in what it consists? Have I verified its presence in the
discerner?[2] If the rightness of the discernment depends principally on
this disposition, then the director's role in verifying its presence is of
corresponding importance.

Ignatius and the early directories divide this disposition into two
parts: the *necessary* disposition and the *helpful* disposition.

The Necessary Disposition

For good discernment, the Official Directory affirms, discerners must
find themselves "in a state of entire availability and equilibrium."[3]

42

This means, Ignatius writes, "that I find myself like a balance at equilibrium, ready to follow whatever I perceive to be more for the glory and praise of God our Lord and the salvation of my soul" (*SpirEx*, 179). This availability, grounded in the foundation—discerners must view their choices as *means* to the *end* for which they are created—is, the Official Directory declares, "extremely important."[4]

Like a balance at equilibrium. Directors must consider questions such as these when judging a discerner's readiness for discernment: Is this young woman who is about to discern between marriage and religious life like a balance at equilibrium, ready to follow whichever choice will be shown to be God's will? Or is she in some measure still closed to one or the other choice? Is she set to some degree on one choice to the practical exclusion of the other? Is this man discerning between a career in medicine or finance like a balance at equilibrium, ready to choose either as it will be shown to be God's will? Or is he in some measure still fixed on one choice and closed to the other?

When directors sense that discerners are not yet like a balance at equilibrium regarding the choices they face, the directors must not invite them to enter the discernment proper, but must dedicate more time to preparation. As Casanovas affirms, the presence or absence of this disposition will principally determine the quality of the discernment. To enter discernment without it leads to prolonged and confused discernments; to enter discernment with it permits progress in the discernment and final clarity.

As directors, we cannot take this availability for granted. At times we see the goodness, the sincere love of God, and the genuine desire to serve God in discerners and may consider that they are ready for discernment. In some instances this may be true. Yet even in such cases—we may think once again of St. Francis Xavier and St. Pierre Favre—Ignatius always led discerners through a preparation to ensure that at least the necessary disposition, if not the further helpful disposition, was present.

As directors, in every case we must explicitly consider whether the discerners are truly available in the choices they face, truly like a balance at equilibrium, or whether their hearts are set in some measure on one option more than the other. If we judge they are not fully available, we must continue the preparation before entering discernment.

Ignatius, who knows the human heart so well, understands the struggle that such availability may cost—for the young woman to be equally available to marriage or religious life, or for the man to be equally available to medicine or finance. Discerners who sincerely desire God's will may find themselves humanly attracted to one choice more than the other.

To assist in such situations, Ignatius invites discerners to ask that God draw them to desire the *opposite* of their present inclination. He writes, "Should the soul be attached and inclined to a thing inordinately, in order that the Creator and Lord may work more certainly in his creature, it is very proper that it move itself with all its strength to desire the opposite of that toward which it is wrongly attached."[5]

One who discerns must seek this grace with energy from God. Ignatius continues, "He should incline his heart to the opposite of his present inclination, being insistent in prayer and other spiritual exercises, and begging of God our Lord for the contrary, that is, that he does not want that office . . . or any other thing unless his Divine Majesty, ordering his desires, should change his former attachment." The conclusion follows: "As a result, the cause of desiring or having one thing or another will be only the service, honor, and glory of his Divine Majesty."[6] Having reached this point, discerners are like a balance at equilibrium, ready for discernment. The Official Directory employs the following comparison: "If you wish to straighten a slender green branch, you bend it in the opposite direction so that remaining midway between the two, it will be straight."[7]

In such cases, the directors' task is to perceive the attachment in the discerners and so the need for such "prayer and spiritual exercises," to present these to discerners, and to accompany their progress toward true availability. Ignatius's insistence on "begging of God our Lord for the contrary" through prayer and spiritual exercises indicates that this progress is not simply a matter of will power; it is a grace to be sought with confidence in God's love. Later in this chapter I will describe this prayer and suggest opportune scriptural texts.

Such availability is necessary before entering discernment.[8] Obviously, once the discernment is complete and discerners know which option is God's will, the time for such availability is past. Then the call is to embrace wholeheartedly that option.

The Helpful Disposition

If the necessary disposition is in place—discerners are now like a balance at equilibrium regarding the options they face—the indispensable preparation for discernment is present. A further disposition, if present, may complete and enrich the necessary disposition. This further disposition, while not indispensable like the necessary disposition, greatly assists discernment when the discerner possesses it.

This additional helpful disposition, Iparraguirre writes, consists in "a positive inclination of heart toward the poverty and humility of Christ,"[9] that is, that in the choice discerners face and before they know which option God wills, they incline more toward the choice that most permits them to live Christ's poverty and humility. This further disposition arises from a love for Christ that awakens a desire to share in his simplicity of life and humble condition.

A young man, for example, is seeking God's will in his vocational discernment. He loves God and sincerely wants to do God's will in the choice he faces. He is close to a young woman and knows that, if he proposes marriage, she will accept. He also has bright prospects for a successful career in business. For years, however, he has felt a call toward priesthood and specifically to a missionary order active in third-world countries. He spent one year as a volunteer with these religious in a developing nation and loved the experience. Now he wonders which calling is God's will.

In order to discern well, he must possess the necessary disposition: he must be like a balance at equilibrium regarding the two choices. If he also possesses the helpful disposition—a positive inclination of heart toward the poverty and humility of Christ—he is ideally prepared to discern. Should he possess this further disposition, the material privations of service in a third-world country will not deter him from embracing this call should it, in the discernment to follow, be revealed as God's will. This further disposition does not mean that he will choose the missionary vocation because in it he will live the poverty and humility of Christ more fully. At this point he does not know which calling is God's will and is ready to accept either once God's will becomes clear. This further disposition does mean that he is so in love with the poor and humble Christ that if God's will should be shown to be the missionary calling, he will be fully ready to embrace it. Because he possesses the further disposition, the privations and humble status of missionary life, compared with a successful business career, will not deter him from accepting this call should it be revealed as God's will.

A woman is discerning between two jobs. She is a professionally skilled teacher and has been offered a position in a prestigious high school in a large city. If she accepts, the salary will permit a comfortable lifestyle and financial security for the future. She has also been offered a position in an inner-city high school for disadvantaged children. The need is great, and resources are few. The salary will be less than in the prestigious high school and the guarantees for the future less certain. This woman also loves God and desires to do God's will in the choice she faces.

In order to discern, she must possess the necessary disposition: she must be like a balance at equilibrium, ready to choose either option should it be revealed as God's will. If she also possesses the helpful disposition—a positive inclination of heart toward the poverty and humility of Christ—she will be ideally prepared to discern. Should the more humble and less remunerative position in the inner-city high school be shown to be God's will, she will be fully prepared to accept this call.

The early sources indicate additional qualities of the disposition that permits discernment. Discernment is greatly helped, Ignatius writes, if the person enters it "with great magnanimity and generosity with his Creator and Lord, offering him all his will and liberty, so that his Divine Majesty may dispose of him and all he possesses according to his most holy will" (*SpirEx*, 5). The person must desire this discernment: one should be admitted to discernment, González Dávila affirms, only if "he requests and desires . . . and is convinced that he ought to deal with this issue."[10] A further directory adds that discerners "should have a very open heart, concealing nothing from the director, neither their desolation nor their consolation."[11]

The Process

How are directors to help discerners acquire this disposition? Ignatius offers two means: contemplation of Christ in the Gospels and meditations directed toward attaining the helpful disposition, the positive inclination of heart toward the poverty and humility of Christ. These means overlap and reinforce each other.

Contemplation of Christ in the Gospels

At this point, discerners have prayed with the foundation and sought freedom from obstacles to discernment. Ignatius now asks directors to invite discerners to contemplate the mysteries of Christ in the Gospels. Specifically, they will contemplate Christ's hidden and public lives (*SpirEx*, 262–88). Such contemplation prepares the discernment and will also accompany it once begun. This contemplation is imaginative: discerners imaginatively see the persons, hear the words, and observe the actions in each mystery of the life of Christ (*SpirEx*, 114–16)—the birth of Jesus (Luke 2:1–20), for example, or the calming of the storm at sea (Matthew 8:23–27).

As they do so, they ask for an "interior knowledge of the Lord . . . so that I may love him more and follow him more closely" (*SpirEx*, 104). Interior knowledge of Christ—a knowledge arising from intimate communion in prayer—deepens love for Christ, and so fosters a readiness to follow him more closely, the goal of this preparation for discernment. As this grace deepens, the discerners' embrace of both the necessary and helpful dispositions will also grow. When this occurs, they have reached the threshold of discernment itself.

Directors must provide discerners appropriate Gospel texts for contemplation. Ignatius supplies them twenty-six such texts. Below I will offer an ample selection of these texts.

Meditations

Ignatius presents four of these: the Call of the Eternal King (*SpirEx*, 91–98), the Two Standards (*SpirEx*, 136–47), the Three Classes (*SpirEx*, 149–57), and the Three Degrees of Humility (*SpirEx*, 164–68). From different perspectives, their common goal is to awaken the helpful disposition in discerners: a love for Christ in his poverty and humility, the desire to live like him, and so a complete availability even to the humanly more demanding option should this be God's will. These meditations may be prayed directly from Ignatius's text, if directors judge opportune, or through scriptural texts that reflect these same themes. Below I will provide a number of such texts.

The Disposition of the Director

At this stage, not only discerners but also their directors, in their specific role, have reached the verge of actual discernment. If discerners require an appropriate disposition for discernment, so also do their directors. The early directories carefully address this point.

The Official Directory counsels that the director "should be kindly rather than austere, especially toward persons suffering from temptations, desolation, aridity, or weariness." Accompanying such persons, the director "ought to console, inspire, and encourage with suitable counsel and advice, as well as by his own and others' prayers." Finally, "It is good if he is liked by the discerner, who will then trust him the more fully and open himself the more freely."[12]

Not only must discerners be like a balance at equilibrium, but their directors also must desire only that God's will be done: "If the director is to execute faithfully the responsibility entrusted to him, he himself must be indifferent [available] in his own way. He must have no other concern or wish than that God's will be done; he must interject nothing of his own spirit, for that would be thrusting his own sickle into God's harvest."[13] The directories warn that if directors pressure discerners toward the choice that the directors desire, only harm will result, "for what is done under constraint will not endure."[14] If directors incline out of personal preferences to pressure discerners toward one choice rather than the other, they must examine this in prayer and, ideally, in some form of supervision.

The directories urge directors to desire earnestly the spiritual profit of the discerners, and to live themselves what they propose to the discerners. "It will help," writes Polanco, "if the director desires with ardent charity to see the discerner's salvation and spiritual progress for the sake of God's glory and out of a wish to see God's will accomplished in him as perfectly as possible."[15] Polanco further invites directors to pray for the discerners throughout the process and especially in moments of particular need. Directors "should beg the prayers of others as well."[16]

The directors, affirms Miró, should themselves meditate briefly on the texts for prayer they will give discerners, "longing and striving with great charity" for their spiritual advancement. They should pray for the discerners and themselves "that the Lord might deign to guide them both."[17]

In serving a discerner, the director is to seek only God's honor and glory. Pereyra elaborates: "For this it would be good that he strive sincerely to have a right intention in this ministry, and not desire or seek in it anything other than what is for the greater honor and glory of the Lord, and for the greater good of that person's soul."[18]

The fruit that discerners will gain, continues Pereyra, depends greatly on the directors, "because it is clear that one who is further advanced and more fervent in the love of God will have greater zeal for the honor of the Lord and the progress of souls, and so will bear more fruit: 'Zeal for your house has consumed me' [Psalm 69:10]."[19]

Such are the dispositions of both discerners and directors that permit fruitful discernment.

Scriptural Texts

I supply here, with some adaptation, a selection of the mysteries of Christ that Ignatius provides in the *Spiritual Exercises*. Directors may choose among these or use others as time allows or as they judge beneficial for individual discerners. As noted earlier, in guiding discerners through these contemplations, directors should invite them to review their prayer in writing and to repeat—the prayer of "repetition" described above—passages in which they experienced notable consolation or desolation, or that touched them in some special way (*SpirEx*, 118). Discerners should pray with these or similar Gospel passages not only during their final preparation for discernment but also during the discernment itself, as we will explain in the following chapters.

Contemplations of Christ in the Gospels

Luke 1:26–38	The annunciation to Mary and incarnation of the Lord.
Luke 1:39–56	The visitation of Mary to Elizabeth.
Luke 2:1–20	The birth of Jesus and the visit of the shepherds.

Luke 2: 22–39	The presentation of Jesus in the temple.
Luke 2:51–52	The hidden life of Jesus in Nazareth.
Luke 2:41–50	Jesus in the temple at twelve years.
Matthew 3:13–17	The baptism of Jesus.
Matthew 4:1–11	Jesus tempted in the desert.
John 1:35–51; Luke 5:1–11; Mark 1:16–20	The call of the apostles.
John 2:1–11	The wedding feast at Cana.
John 2:13–22	Jesus casts the buyers and sellers from the temple.
Matthew 5:1–48	The Sermon on the Mount.
Matthew 8:23–27	Jesus calms the storm.
Matthew 10:1–16	The apostles sent out to preach.
Luke 7:36–50	The woman who washes the feet of Jesus.
Matthew 14:13–21	The feeding of the five thousand.
Matthew 14:22–33	Jesus walks on the water.
Matthew 17:1–9	The transfiguration.
John 11:1–45	The raising of Lazarus.
Matthew 26:6–10	The supper at Bethany.
Matthew 21:1–17	Palm Sunday.

Meditations for Seeking the Helpful Disposition

The following scriptural texts will aid discerners to pray for the helpful disposition, the positive inclination of heart toward the poverty and humility of Christ. According to the director's judgment, some or all of these may be prayed together at a given time. They may also be interspersed among the contemplations of the events in Christ's life as listed above.

Matthew 20:20–28	Like Jesus: not to be served but to serve.
John 10:1–18	Like the good shepherd who lays down his life for his sheep.
Matthew 16:24–27	The condition for following Jesus.
1 Corinthians 4:9–13	Fools for Christ.
Philippians 2:1–11	Have the mind of Christ.
Philippians 3:3–16	Whatever gain I had I counted as loss.

Luke 9:57–62	Complete availability to follow Jesus.
Luke 18:18–30	The freedom to answer Jesus' call.
Luke 1:38;	
Matthew 4:18–22;	
Matthew 13:44–46	A wholehearted yes to God.
2 Corinthians 6:1–13	Sharing in the cross of Christ.
Galatians 6:14	My glory is the cross of Christ.

Thus far in this book, we have discussed the preparation that guides discerners to the disposition necessary for discernment. We turn now to that discernment itself.

Chapter Five

Clarity beyond Doubting

The First Mode

*This is when the will of God is shown so clearly that no
doubt regarding it is possible.*

—Official Directory

Discerners have now reached the heart of the process, the time of
discernment itself. Their directors have judged that the discerners'
preparation is sufficient: the foundation has been adequately assimilated, the obstacles largely removed, and the disposition essentially
acquired. The discerners are ready to discern.

Throughout the weeks and, if necessary and time allows, the
months to follow, discerners will continue to pray daily. They will
contemplate Christ in the Gospels each day, seeking that deepened
interior knowledge of the Lord that allows them to love and follow
him more closely. Simultaneously, they will strive for that positive
inclination of heart toward the poverty and humility of Christ that
best disposes them to discern. Discerners will review this prayer daily.
They will also review the spiritual experience of the entire day through
the examen prayer. In regular meetings with their directors, they will
share the content of this review and examen: the spiritual consolations and desolations they have experienced, the attractions and resistances, the different thoughts—the entire spiritual experience related
to their discernment. Their directors will help them understand what
is and what is not of God in this experience, and, based upon what
emerges in the discerners' experience, suggest appropriate scriptural
texts for prayer.

God has promised that if we seek we shall find (Matt 7:7). From
long experience, his own and that of others whom he aided, Ignatius

identified three patterns or modes in the way God responds to discerners engaged in the process just described. In the first, God makes his will so clear that no doubt is possible. Our task here is to describe this mode and the director's role in it.

First-Mode Discernment: What Is It?

We will approach this mode first through Ignatius's own experience, the origin of his understanding regarding it.[1] After his conversion, Ignatius spent many months in the town of Manresa, a time of penitential rigor. Among the ascetical practices he adopted was total abstinence from meat. In his autobiography, Ignatius described the experience that altered this resolve:

> While he [Ignatius] was persevering in his abstinence from eating meat, and was so firm in this that he had no thought of changing, one day in the morning, when he had risen, some meat prepared for eating was represented to him, as though he saw it with his bodily eyes, without his having any desire for it beforehand. At the same time there came to him a great assent of the will that from then on he should eat it. And although he remembered his former intention, he could not doubt about the matter, but resolved that he ought to eat meat. Relating this afterward to his confessor, the confessor told him that he should consider whether this might not be a temptation. But he, examining it well, could never doubt about this.[2]

In this experience, *something is shown* to Ignatius: that God does not want him to continue in a specific penitential practice. In the same moment, *Ignatius's will is strongly drawn* to what is shown him: "There came to him a great assent of the will that from then on he should eat it." Finally, Ignatius simply *cannot doubt* that what is shown him is God's will: "And although he remembered his former intention, he could not doubt about the matter. . . . But he, examining it well, could never doubt about this."

Reflection on such experiences led Ignatius to identify a first "time"—that is, a first way, a first mode[3]—through which God may reveal his will in choices between good options. Ignatius describes this mode succinctly in the *Spiritual Exercises*:

The first time is when God our Lord so moves and attracts the will that, without doubting or being able to doubt, the devout soul follows what is shown to it, as St. Paul and St. Matthew did in following Christ our Lord (*SpirEx*, 175).[4]

In this brief text, Ignatius formulates a general teaching drawn from experiences like that described. Here we again find the same three elements:

- something is shown to a person ("the devout soul follows *what is shown* to it")
- the person's will is drawn to what is shown ("God our Lord *so moves and attracts the will*")
- and the person cannot doubt that what is shown and what so draws the will is truly God's will ("*without doubting or being able to doubt*").

Such experiences, Ignatius writes, are a first way in which God may reveal his will to those who must choose between good options.[5]

In the text just cited, Ignatius offers two biblical examples of first-mode discernment: the conversion of St. Paul (Acts 9:1–9) and the call of St. Matthew (Matt 9:9). In both he perceives the three elements just described.

When Paul undergoes his experience of conversion, *something is shown* to him: that Jesus is Lord and is calling him to be his apostle. Paul's *will is completely drawn* to what is shown him: his whole being says a total "yes" to this call. And Paul *cannot doubt* then or ever that Jesus called him to be his apostle. Ignatius sees here an experience of first-mode discernment.

Likewise the experience of Matthew. *Something is shown* to Matthew: his calling to follow Jesus as his disciple. Matthew's *will is fully drawn* to what is shown him: his whole being says a total "yes" to this call. And Matthew *cannot doubt* then or ever that Jesus called him to be his apostle. Here again, Ignatius perceives an experience of first-mode discernment.[6]

How does first-mode discernment appear in practice? And how does a director accompany such discernment? A review of experiences from real life will help answer these questions.

First-Mode Discernment in Practice: Experiences

The reader will note that, like the biblical examples Ignatius provides, all of the following experiences concern vocational calls. In my reading and in many interviews with persons who shared their discernments, the clearest instances of first-mode discernment that I encountered regarded vocational choices.[7] For that reason, in an exposition intended to provide clarity, I offer them here. Obviously this does not signify that first-mode discernment may be experienced only in vocational discernment. Ignatius's discernment regarding the penitential practice underscores this point.[8]

We will first review experiences in which first-mode discernment occurs dramatically. We will then examine others in which such discernment takes place more quietly.

Anne's Experience

In the account that follows, I have highlighted key elements for our reflection on first-mode discernment:

> A religious experience occurred in November of Anne's senior year of high school. Religious life as a lifestyle had never been a consideration for her. She remembers asking out of curiosity what kind of woman could become a nun. After naming some qualifications, sister turned to Anne and said, "Someone like you. You could become a sister." Anne's response was a definite and silent, "No way!" Anne also recalls praying intensely to God and expressing her desire to do whatever he wanted her to do EXCEPT become a nun. These were the only times the subject ever came up, and they were soon forgotten.
>
> It happened on a Sunday morning, the last day of a weekend retreat made by the seniors. Anne had stopped to make a visit in the chapel. As she began to kneel down, she experienced a powerful shock—like a lightning bolt that went straight through her from head to feet. She felt *her whole being lifted up in a surging "yes!"* She had no control over it. It was much like riding the crest of a wave—one must go with it. There were no images, no words, no arguments, *no doubts,*

no reasoning process to make. It was decided—period! She knelt there a few seconds absorbing the impact. There was a sense of great peace and joy and direction. In fact, it was the only time she had ever experienced *such certitude.*

Along with the call to religious life was also the name of the religious community. All that was needed was for Anne to follow through on the decision.

The decision was tested many times. In the course of the year *the certitude never changed*, neither did the deep inner peace and joy. . . .

It was *this certitude* and deep peace that carried her through the year, enabled her to leave home, and helped her weather the homesickness and discouragement of the novitiate. For years after, Anne would feel the powerful impact of the experience whenever she recalled it. It was a gift, and she confesses that she would never have made it [through those years] without it. It gave her a basic joyous outlook and confidence in life and the secure sense of being loved by God—a love that she could feel in a tangible way. In her late thirties, Anne went through a period of spiritual desolation. Part of the desolation, the most painful part, was the loss of that sense of God's loving presence. And yet, in the midst of the confusion, guilt, and emptiness, the certitude of her vocation was left unshaken. *It could not be doubted*—when she had to believe that God was there, she knew he had chosen her to be his as a religious.

As she reflects on this, she believes that certitude comes from the fact that essentially the decision was God's; she only freely consented to accept it, to ride along on the crest of it.[9]

As she stops in the chapel, God simply showers grace upon Anne. She searches for images to express the abundance of the gift: a powerful shock, a lightning bolt, the crest of a wave.

In this experience, *something is shown* to Anne: the call to religious life and, with it, "also the name of the religious community." In the power of the experience, *Anne's will is attracted and moved* toward what is shown her: "She felt her whole being lifted up in a surging 'yes!'" And Anne *cannot doubt* that what is shown and what so attracts her is truly God's will: "There were . . . no arguments, no doubts, no reasoning process to make. . . . It was the only time she had ever experienced such certitude. . . . The certitude never changed. . . . It could not be doubted." Clearly, Anne's vocational discernment occurs according to the first mode Ignatius outlines in his *Spiritual Exercises*.

As with Ignatius's experience regarding the penitential practice, Anne undergoes no extended process of discernment. She simply receives complete clarity as a gift from God; her part is to accept the gift and act upon it.[10] This Anne unhesitatingly does, as the account indicates: "All that was needed was for Anne to follow through on the decision," and, in fact, "she . . . freely consented to accept it."

God's gift on that Sunday morning sustains Anne throughout her entire religious life: "For years after, Anne would feel the powerful impact of the experience whenever she recalled it. . . . It gave her a basic joyous outlook and confidence in life and the secure sense of being loved by God." When desolation arises, this experience continues to support Anne.

What is the director's part here? When an Anne speaks with her director, for what does her director look? What questions may need to be asked?

As directors listen to an account like Anne's, they will watch to see if the three elements of first-mode discernment are present and with sufficient clarity. What *has been shown* to Anne? Two things are shown to her that Sunday morning: her call to religious life and the specific religious community she is to join. Directors must note with care exactly what has been shown in the experience. Only that which has been shown in the experience may be clearly understood to be God's will. As we will see, even in first-mode vocational discernment, the second element—the call to a specific religious community or to a diocese—may not always be shown.

Directors will also be attentive to observe if the person experiences *a strong and unifying attraction of the will* toward what is shown. Does everything in this person say "yes" to what is shown? Like Ignatius and the penitential practice? Like Paul and Matthew? Like Anne in this account? If the person's will resists in some measure, directors must question whether true first-mode discernment is present and whether, therefore, God's will has been found. At times this full assent of the will may be accompanied by fear of actually taking the step. Such fear does not negate the first-mode discernment. In these cases, directors will help the persons overcome their fear and put their discernment into practice.

Finally, directors will note whether the person simply *cannot doubt* that what has been shown is God's will. In true first-mode discernment, the person does not doubt and cannot doubt that this is so, both when the experience occurs and after.[11] Such clarity is evident in Anne's experience and sustains her throughout her life. If, on the other hand, directors find that the person employs expressions of this nature, "It was a powerful experience, a great grace, and I am so grateful for it. I am almost sure now that I have found God's will," or, "When I had that experience last week I was sure that God had shown me his will, although since then I've sometimes wondered," then first-mode discernment has not occurred. The experience is very likely important in the discernment and should be considered well. It is not first-mode discernment, however, and the process of discernment must continue.

Mark's Experience

From an early age, Mark desired to be a priest.[12] Because he knew diocesan priesthood best, Mark presumed that this was his call. He pursued diocesan priesthood and was happy with this process. Still, a question about a call to religious priesthood—to be a Franciscan, Dominican, or Benedictine—lingered. When Mark raised this question in spiritual direction, the director encouraged him to continue his process with the diocese unless God should "knock you off your horse on the way to Damascus."

Mark recounts what followed:

> This was my last year of high school. On January 29, during civics class, my friend Mitchell mentioned in passing that a former teacher of ours said that I should become a Jesuit. Mitchell and I laughed at that, but I thought little more about it. I was already halfway through my application process for

the diocesan seminary and was content with this path. During English class, my classmates and I were in the library making note cards for our research papers when the strangest thing happened: I was suddenly overwhelmed with excitement over the prospect of becoming a Jesuit. This was extraordinary, given that (a) all of this was happening in a public school; (b) I wasn't, at that moment, in a state of prayer; and (c) I hardly knew what a Jesuit was! Though no exterior vision or miraculous event had occurred, I sensed that a tectonic shift had just rocked my whole world. . . .

Later that day, I went directly to my spiritual director and said, "Do you remember when you told me to tell God to knock me off my horse if he wants me to do something else? Well, I think I've just got knocked off my horse!"

Days later, being completely unable to shake this obsession with a group I knew practically nothing about, I took my spiritual director's advice and called the nearest Jesuit community. When Father Madden answered the phone, I asked, "May I speak to a Jesuit, please? Anyone will do." A few days later I met with him. A few weeks later, I applied to the Jesuits, and a few months later, I was in the novitiate. I have never looked back.

Mark shares his belief that "this extraordinary moment was from God and that God, for his own reasons, wanted me to skip the ordinarily necessary phases and move right to the near end of the discernment process." Mark notes that Ignatius says of such experiences "that one is 'without being able to doubt,'" and that is exactly how I felt. In all the discernments I have made since, I cannot recall ever having such a moment of absolute clarity." Wisely, after this experience, Mark speaks with his spiritual director, undergoes a "rigorous application process with the Jesuits," and lives the two-year experience of the novitiate before taking vows as a Jesuit.

Spiritual directors, hearing this account, will recognize that the elements of first-mode discernment appear to be present. *Something is shown* to Mark: his call to be a Jesuit. He experiences a *strong assent of the will*: "I was suddenly overwhelmed with excitement over the prospect of becoming a Jesuit." And Mark is *not able to doubt*

that this was God's call: "one is 'without being able to doubt,' and
that is exactly how I felt."

For the director, everything said in regard to verifying Anne's
experience as true first-mode discernment applies once more. In conversation with Mark, the director will note whether Mark clearly perceived a call to be a Jesuit, whether his "overwhelming excitement" at
this prospect was truly a full assent of the will, whether the "moment
of absolute clarity" excluded any doubt, and whether this clarity has
endured since the experience.

Margaret's Experience

Margaret is exploring a call to religious life. At this point, her discernment clarifies:

> Finally at the close of the semester, the answer came suddenly
> and stopped all questioning. "For you the . . . cloistered life
> is the way to give me everything. Others can do this in other
> ways, but this is to be your way." These may not have been
> the exact words, but the message was unmistakable. There
> was never another question or doubt before or after the Sisters
> accepted me into the . . . community.[13]

Less is said in this account than in Anne's and Mark's. To determine whether Margaret's experience is true first-mode discernment,
directors will need to hear Margaret speak more amply about it.
Something is in fact *shown* to her: her call to cloistered religious life.
Is she also shown the specific monastic community? Margaret does
not answer this question explicitly in her account. Directors, aware of
this, will invite Margaret to describe the experience more fully, attentive to what she may say about the community.

Does Margaret give a *full assent of the will* to this call? Such may
be implied when Margaret tells us that the experience "stopped all
questioning." Here too, directors will help Margaret to speak more
amply and so determine whether such assent is in fact present in the
experience.

Margaret does indicate clearly that she *cannot doubt* the call to
cloistered life: the call stops all questioning, is unmistakable, and

"There was never another question or doubt before or after the Sisters accepted me into the . . . community." As she speaks, directors will note Margaret's strong and lasting conviction regarding this element of first-mode discernment.

Margaret's experience, therefore, may well be a first-mode discernment. Directors, hearing brief accounts of this nature, must learn more about the experience in order to judge whether this is so.

The experiences related thus far describe first-mode discernment in dramatic circumstances: the individual receives clarity in a given moment, generally unexpected and simply received as a gift of God's love. As the following experiences indicate, first-mode discernment may occur in quieter ways as well.[14]

Gary's Experience

In the narrative related here, Gary describes his discernment of priesthood. I have highlighted the key elements for first-mode discernment:

> I would find it hard to say exactly when my calling as a priest first became clear to me. It was always there, in a sense. It was there as far back as I can remember thinking about my future, certainly already when I was in grade school. Faith was an important part of our family life, and we were always active in the parish. Catholic school also helped. So the spiritual soil for a vocation was there, though I was the only one of the three boys in the family who felt this call.
>
> There was never any struggle about my vocation, never any searching to see whether God wanted me to be a priest. *It was just clear to me and has always been clear to me since.* I always had great esteem for marriage, and my parents were great examples, but I knew that it wasn't my call. I remember reading one of Thomas Merton's books once, and feeling all of this very strongly; *I just longed to be a priest and live that life. It was all I wanted.*
>
> In my last year in college, when I had to decide what I would do, there was, in a sense, no decision to make: *I knew that God wanted me to be a priest.* I didn't know whether God wanted me to be a diocesan priest or a religious priest,

and I spent that year looking into the diocese and several religious communities until I found my answer, and entered the diocese.

I remember that when my ordination as deacon was about six months away, my spiritual director said that I needed to think well about it since this was the definitive commitment. I was willing to reflect but I knew, in my heart, that it was already clear. *It had always been clear.* It still is today, after thirty-seven years of priesthood.

For me, really, the only issue has always been fidelity to the calling, living it well, and never whether God called me to priesthood or not. *I've never doubted that, and I can't doubt it.* I've always been grateful to God for that.

Directors will hear the elements of first-mode discernment in this account: all three are unmistakably present. *Something is shown* to Gary: "I knew that God wanted me to be a priest." Gary's *will fully assents* to this call: "I just longed to be a priest and live that life. It was all I wanted." And Gary *cannot doubt* this call: "I've never doubted that, and I can't doubt it." In an undramatic way and with a clarity perceived from early years, Gary experiences first-mode discernment in regard to his priestly vocation. When Gary speaks with a spiritual director, the director will recognize the elements of first-mode discernment and will confirm that Gary has discerned well his call.

We may note that while *what is shown* to Anne concerns both her call to religious life and the specific community to which God calls her, the same is not true for Gary. Gary's clarity concerns his call to priesthood; he does not have first-mode clarity in regard to *where* God wills him to become a priest—whether in his diocese or in a religious community, and if this latter, in which specific community. With respect to where God is calling him to be a priest, Gary must continue to discern in the normal way: if he is drawn to diocesan priesthood, he will speak with his diocesan vocation director and visit the seminary; if he is attracted to religious priesthood, he will speak with the institute's vocation director and visit the community. Such comparison between Anne's and Gary's experiences highlights the need to grasp clearly "what is shown" in first-mode discernment.

Georg's Experience

Father Georg Ratzinger, the brother of Benedict XVI, discerned his calling much like Gary. Again I have highlighted key elements for first-mode discernment:

> I can no longer say exactly when I first heard *the call to the priesthood*, for actually *it had always been clear to me* that that was where my destiny lay. When I was an altar boy and served Mass, *I already knew* that that would be my place: now I was an acolyte, but later I myself would have the privilege of standing in the priest's place. *I never doubted* it for a moment; it all happened naturally, in an almost organic development. I never really had to think about it, *so sure was I* of my vocation. . . .
>
> I . . . *never had to wrestle with myself* and did not need to make a difficult decision. Actually *it was clear to me from the beginning*—although serving at the altar and, of course, perhaps more than anything else, the spirituality of our family had something to do with it—that I would go into ministry. For me, that was *always something self-evident*.[15]

Two of the three elements are explicitly expressed in this account: *something is shown*—the call to the priesthood—and Georg repeats many times his *inability to doubt the call*. The full *assent of the will* is expressed less clearly—"I never had to wrestle with myself"—though it may be implied from the serene surety of the entire account. Nonetheless, hearing Georg's description, a director will gently invite him to speak more directly about whether he deeply desires what has been shown to him so clearly.

First-Mode Discernment: The Director's Role

As the experiences related indicate, first-mode discernment is a freely given gift of God. Consequently—by contrast with second- and third-mode discernment—there is no formal process by which to seek it.

Directors may briefly explain first-mode discernment to discerners, will help them acquire the disposition necessary for discernment according to any mode God may choose, and then will watch to see whether God gives first-mode clarity. Little more need be said to discerners about first-mode discernment unless God should grant this gift.[16]

The directories indicate that directors may explain first-mode discernment but only briefly. Polanco writes that "the director should explain the first mode in passing."[17] González Dávila affirms that "there is little to say about the first mode because it is extraordinary and falls under no rule,"[18] and the Official Directory advises that "regarding the first mode little needs to be said."[19] Thus, directors may inform discerners that God may choose to reveal his will through a clarity beyond doubting, but should do so without length or special emphasis.

Such brevity reflects the fact that, as González Dávila notes, first-mode discernment is simply a gift of God's grace and that no process can prepare specifically for it. There is, consequently, little to explain. Among some commentators, as González Dávila's comments also illustrate, this restraint likewise reflects a view that first-mode discernment is less common—for the Official Directory it is "out of the ordinary" and "rare"[20]—than second- or third-mode discernment. Others—and I find myself among them—while agreeing that first-mode discernment occurs less frequently than the second or third mode, also know from experience that it can occur, and that therefore directors must be prepared to identify it should God give it.[21] Views like those of the Official Directory, however, wisely caution directors not to reach this judgment precipitously.

When discerners present an experience that they consider first-mode discernment—"God has made this so clear that I cannot doubt it is his will"—directors must note carefully whether this experience is true first-mode discernment or whether it may be the product of the discerners' imagination, of their lack of experience in the spiritual life, or of disordered affections that affect their judgment in varying degrees. With good will and perhaps influenced by subjective considerations, discerners may judge too quickly that a certain experience is first-mode discernment.[22] Thus, regardless of how clear the discernment may appear to discerners, they must always speak with their directors and receive their directors' confirmation.[23] Serious and damaging errors may otherwise occur. The directors' responsibility is evident.

When they have explained first-mode discernment to discerners, directors will invite them to begin second-mode discernment and, should this not bring clarity, the third mode as well. As discerners engage in these modes, directors will watch to see whether God, in a given moment, may grant the grace of first-mode discernment. Should they judge, after carefully listening to the discerners' experience and after appropriate reflection, that God has done so, the discernment is concluded. If not, they will continue to accompany discerners through discernment in the second and third modes.

First-Mode Discernment: A Director's Checklist

When directors assist discerners in judging whether God has given them first-mode discernment, questions such as these will assist them:

- *What specifically was shown* to the person? Was it, as with Anne, both a calling to religious life and to a precise religious community? Or, as with Gary, simply the calling to priesthood without further specification? In the experience, what *specifically* did God show the one discerning?
- In the experience, *was there a clear attraction and drawing of the will* toward what was shown? Was there, as with Ignatius, "a great assent of the will"? As with Anne, "a surging 'yes!'"? As with Gary, a single-hearted drawing—"It was all I wanted"?
- *Was it truly impossible for the person to doubt* that this discernment was of God? Like Ignatius, who "could never doubt" his discernment about a penitential practice? Like Anne, whose discernment "could not be doubted" through all the vicissitudes of life? Like Georg, whose calling "had always been clear to me"? Has this certitude remained after the initial experience?
- *Has the one discerning spoken with you* about the experience? Discernment, even in this first mode, must never be done in isolation.

- Finally, if this is authentic first-mode discernment, *has the recipient of this gift acted upon it?*

In his *Autograph Directory*, Ignatius writes, "Among the three modes of making a discernment, if God does not move the person in the first mode, he should apply himself to the second."[24] We turn now to that second mode.

Chapter Six

An Attraction of the Heart
The Second Mode (I)

Let him note, when he is in consolation, to which part God moves him.

—St. Ignatius of Loyola

Because first-mode discernment is simply a gift of God, no specific steps can prepare discerners for it. Their part, with the aid of their directors, is to enter the process of discernment with generosity, seeking the disposition and faithfully using the means: daily prayer with Scripture, review of this prayer, the examen, and the other means already described. If God chooses to grant first-mode clarity during the process, they will receive with gratitude God's loving gift.

But directors cannot presume that God will give this gift. Their part, once discerners have acquired the necessary disposition, is to guide them into second-mode discernment. Ignatius describes this mode succinctly in his *Spiritual Exercises*: "The second is when sufficient clarity and understanding is received through experience of consolations and desolations, and through experience of discernment of different spirits" (*SpirEx*, 176).

In this densely worded text, Ignatius names two experiences: the *experience of consolations and desolations*, and the *experience of discernment of different spirits*. In second-mode discernment, Ignatius says, through these two experiences discerners receive "sufficient clarity and understanding" in their discernments, that is, they receive all the clarity and understanding they need to know which option God wills for them. A review of these two experiences will clarify the nature of second-mode discernment.

Experience of Consolations and Desolations

In second-mode discernment, Ignatius focuses on *spiritual consolation* and *spiritual desolation* (*SpirEx*, 316–17). *Spiritual consolation* is a happy, uplifting movement of the heart (and so, "consolation") on the level of faith and of our relationship with God (and so, "spiritual").[1] In the following time of prayer, Raïssa Maritain, wife of the philosopher Jacques Maritain, experiences specifically *spiritual consolation*. She begins to pray the Litany of the Sacred Heart of Jesus and never moves past the first three words, *Kyrie eleison*, Lord have mercy. She writes:

> At the first invocation, *Kyrie eleison*, obliged to absorb myself, my mind arrested on the Person of the Father. Impossible to change the object. Sweetness, attraction, *eternal youth* of the heavenly Father. Suddenly, keen sense of his nearness, of his tenderness, of his incomprehensible love which impels him to demand our love, our thought. Greatly moved, I wept very sweet tears. . . . Joy of being able to call him Father with a great tenderness, to feel him so kind and so close to me.[2]

We sense immediately that we are on holy ground here, and we approach this experience with reverence. In her prayer, Raïssa experiences *consolation*—an uplifting movement of the heart. Her heart feels warmth, tenderness, joy, and sweetness. The joy of her heart is expressed even physically in "very sweet tears." Raïssa's heart is richly *consoled*.

And her consolation is clearly *spiritual*—on the level of faith and of her relationship with God. The source of her joy is "the Person of the Father," her "keen sense of his nearness, of his tenderness, of his incomprehensible love," and her feeling of him "so kind and so close to me." All of this is on the *spiritual* level. In second-mode discernment, Ignatius teaches, directors help discerners note such experiences of spiritual consolation and the attraction toward one option or the other that they feel during these experiences.

The adjective "spiritual" with which Ignatius carefully prefaces the term "consolation" indicates that not all uplifting movements of the heart are included in second-mode discernment.[3] The human person also experiences uplifting movements of the heart on the natural and human level—on the *nonspiritual* level. Persons, for example, who exercise in a healthy manner, enjoy a good meal with friends, listen to beautiful music, gaze at the ocean, or successfully accomplish a task, feel good: their hearts are uplifted. Such natural joys are a blessing of the Creator, and we rightfully appreciate them. But they are not the *spiritual* consolation that Ignatius intends in second-mode discernment.[4]

When discerners share their spiritual experiences, directors must note whether the consolations described are spiritual or nonspiritual, and so whether or not they pertain to second-mode discernment. If, for example, Raïssa were engaged in a process of discernment and during her time of spiritual consolation were drawn to one of the options, that drawing would pertain richly to second-mode discernment. Should directors fail to distinguish between nonspiritual and spiritual consolation when discerners describe their experiences, they risk leading discerners astray in second-mode discernment.

Spiritual desolation is the exact contrary of spiritual consolation. Spiritual desolation is a heavy, discouraging movement of the heart (and so, "desolation") on the level of faith and of our relationship with God (and so, "spiritual"). Jane is making an Ignatian retreat. The first three days have been filled with a joyful awareness of God's deeply personal love for her—they have been days of spiritual consolation. The joy of those days, however, leads Jane to increase her times of prayer, stretching her energies too far. By day six, Jane experiences specifically *spiritual desolation*:

> Day 4: Jane gets up with a bad headache, feeling exhausted and under strain. She cannot pray well. All joy has evaporated. She is tired and sad and moody. Finally, in the evening she tells the director about her action of the previous day and its results. The director advises cutting down on prayer time and resting more.
>
> Day 5: She follows the advice, prays less, but still has no enthusiasm and is filled with gloom.
>
> Day 6: At her morning prayer she becomes very much disturbed. She begins to doubt the Lord's presence to her even

in the opening days of the retreat. Probably, she thinks, she
should attribute everything to her overactive imagination.
Who is she to be given a taste of the sweetness of the Lord?
She begins to grow discouraged at the thought that she is not
meant for a deep prayer life. Her desire for God is just an illusion. The rest of the day is one of disquietude, confusion, and
a sense of discouragement.[5]

Again we approach this spiritual experience with reverence. On
day six, Jane experiences *desolation*—a heavy movement of the
heart. Her heart is disturbed, begins to doubt, and is discouraged,
disquieted, and confused. Jane's heart is deeply *desolate*.

And her desolation is clearly *spiritual*—on the level of faith and
of her relationship with God. Jane now doubts the Lord's presence
to her in the earlier days of spiritual consolation, considers herself
unworthy to taste the sweetness of the Lord, feels that she is not
meant for a deep prayer life, and judges that her desire for God is just
an illusion. All of this is on the *spiritual* level. In second-mode discernment, Ignatius teaches, directors help discerners note such experiences of spiritual desolation and the attraction toward one option
or the other they feel while experiencing them.

As a parallel to spiritual consolation, the adjective "spiritual" with
which Ignatius prefaces the term "desolation" indicates that not all
heavy movements of the heart are included in second-mode discernment. The human person also experiences heavy movements of the
heart on the natural and human level—on the *nonspiritual* level. A
man, for example, works late repeatedly and rises early; eventually
a heaviness enters his life due to the depletion of his physical energy.
A woman who hears a disparaging remark in her regard may feel
discouraged; a heaviness enters her life due to a depletion of her emotional energy. Such experiences are significant and require appropriate remedies. But they are not the *spiritual* desolation that Ignatius
intends in second-mode discernment.

When discerners share their spiritual experiences, directors must
also note whether any desolations described are spiritual or nonspiritual and so whether or not they pertain to second-mode discernment. If, for example, Jane were engaged in a process of discernment

and during her spiritually desolate day six were drawn to one of the options, that drawing would pertain to second-mode discernment.

We may note that Jane's experience of *spiritual* desolation on day six is prepared by an experience of *nonspiritual* desolation on day four. On the third day, Jane stretches her energies too far and consequently awakens on day four "with a bad headache, feeling exhausted and under strain." Her nonspiritual desolation is the space into which the enemy brings the further trap of spiritual desolation: now, on day six, Jane doubts God's presence to her and considers her desire for closeness with God illusory. An exact parallel exists with *consolation*. Often, in God's providence, experiences of healthy *nonspiritual* consolation are the space into which God infuses the further gift of *spiritual* consolation: a woman, for example, enjoys watching a beautiful sunset and, as she does so, her heart is warmed with the surety of God's powerful and faithful love for her.

In second-mode discernment, Ignatius asks that directors attend carefully to the discerners' *experience of consolations and desolations.*

Experience of Discernment of Different Spirits

The second experience that permits second-mode discernment is, Ignatius says, the "experience of discernment of different spirits." Presuming the first experience, that is, that discerners are experiencing spiritual consolations and spiritual desolations as they continue in the process, the *different spirits*—that is, the good spirit and the enemy—at work in such consolation and desolation must be *discerned.*[6] It is this experience of discerning the work of the good spirit and the enemy in the spiritual consolations and desolations discerners undergo that permits second-mode discernment. A look at three texts in Ignatius's writings will clarify this experience of discerning different spirits.

The Autograph Directory

In his notes for directors entitled the *Autograph Directory,* Ignatius describes second-mode discernment at greater length:

Among the three modes of making a choice, if God does not
move a person in the first mode, one should dwell persistently
on the second, that of recognizing his vocation by the experience of consolations and desolations; in such manner that,
as he continues with his meditations of Christ our Lord, he
observes, when he finds himself in consolation, to which part
God moves him, and likewise when he finds himself in desolation. And what consolation is should be well explained; that
is, spiritual joy, love, hope in things of above, tears, and every
interior movement that leaves the soul consoled in our Lord.
The contrary of this is desolation: sadness, lack of confidence,
lack of love, dryness, etc.[7]

Again Ignatius qualifies second-mode discernment as an "experience of consolations and desolations": such discernment presumes
that a discerner is experiencing times of spiritual consolation and
spiritual desolation "as he continues with his meditations of Christ
our Lord," that is, as he prays daily in the time of discernment.

As the discerner experiences these spiritual movements, "he
observes, when he finds himself in consolation, to which part God
moves him, and likewise when he finds himself in desolation." That
is to say, when he finds himself in *spiritual consolation*, he observes
toward which of the options *God* is drawing him; and when he finds
himself in *spiritual desolation*, he observes toward which of the
options the *enemy* is drawing him. He continues to note attentively
these drawings in spiritual consolation and spiritual desolation as the
days go by.

If God is in fact calling him to second-mode discernment, a pattern
will emerge over time: when he experiences spiritual consolation, he
will find himself consistently drawn to one option; when, on the other
hand, he experiences spiritual desolation, he may find his drawing
toward that option attacked and experience a drawing toward the
other option. In this case, both the consistent drawing by God in spiritual consolation toward one option and the attack on this drawing by
the enemy in spiritual desolation confirm the second-mode discernment. This discerner now has "sufficient clarity and understanding"
in his discernment and knows which option God wills.

Ignatius reminds directors that "what consolation is should be well explained" as also should desolation. Evidently, if God calls discerners to second-mode discernment, they must know what both spiritual consolation and spiritual desolation are. Without this knowledge, they will not hear God's will as revealed through the second mode. Consequently, Ignatius says, their directors must explain these well to them.[8]

The Spirits in the First Set of Rules

In his first set of rules for the discernment of spirits, Ignatius enunciates a truth that underlies second-mode discernment:

> As in consolation the good spirit guides and counsels us more, so in desolation the bad spirit, with whose counsels we cannot find the way to a right decision (*SpirEx*, 318).

In the discernment Ignatius describes in this rule, the *good spirit* guides discerners when they experience *spiritual consolation*: that is, when in time of spiritual consolation discerners feel drawn toward one option, they know that the good spirit is counseling them—that God is drawing them to that option. When, on the other hand, discerners experience *spiritual desolation*, the *enemy* is guiding them: that is, when in time of spiritual desolation they feel drawn toward one option, they know that the enemy is counseling them—that God, therefore, does not want that option.

In the situation Ignatius envisages in the second set of rules for the discernment of spirits (*SpirEx*, 328–36), this situation will change. We will examine this different situation in the following chapter.

Through the texts cited, Ignatius has prepared us to approach second-mode discernment. We may now explore this discernment in his own experience.

Radical or Mitigated Poverty?

Ignatius is fifty-two years old, the head of the Company of Jesus.[9] He is writing the Constitutions for the Company of Jesus and is discerning God's will regarding the poverty that he and his companions will live: Does God will them to live in radical poverty, with no fixed revenue at all? Or does God will some mitigation of this poverty for the good of the churches entrusted to their care? Ignatius decides to celebrate Mass on forty consecutive days to seek light from God in a discernment that he knows will affect many lives. On Saturday, February 2, 1544, Ignatius begins the forty days. In his *Spiritual Diary* he writes the following:

> 1. Saturday—Deep devotion at Mass, with tears and increased confidence in Our Lady, and more inclination to complete poverty then and throughout the day.

Ignatius describes similar experiences on the following days:

> 2. Sunday—The same, and more inclination to no revenue then, and throughout the day.
>
> 3. Monday—The same, and with other feelings, and more inclined to no revenue throughout the day. . . .
>
> 4. Tuesday—An abundance of devotion before Mass, during it and after it, tears. . . . I . . . felt more inclined to perfect poverty at the time and throughout the day. . . .
>
> 5. Wednesday—Devotion before Mass and during it, not without tears, more inclined to perfect poverty. . . .
>
> 6. Thursday—Before Mass with deep devotion and tears, and a notable warmth and devotion all through the day, being always moved more to perfect poverty.[10]

Later in the process, however, more troubling experiences enter. On the fortieth day, Ignatius writes:

> When the Mass was finished and I was in my room afterward, I found myself utterly deserted and without any help, unable to feel the presence of my mediators[11] or of the Divine Persons, but feeling so remote and so separated from them as if I had never felt their presence and never would again.[12]

In this time of darkness, new thoughts arise:

Thoughts came to me at times against Jesus, at times against another Person, finding myself confused with various thoughts such as to leave the house and rent a room in order to get away from the noise, or to fast, or to begin the Masses all over again, or to move the altar to a higher floor in the house. I could find rest in nothing, desiring to end in a time of consolation and with my heart totally satisfied.

In Ignatius's description, the *experience of consolations and desolations* is abundantly verified. The first days are filled with *spiritual consolation*: in them, Ignatius experiences deep devotion at Mass, warmth, tears, and increased confidence in Our Lady's intercession. Later, however, he experiences notable *spiritual desolation*: Ignatius feels utterly deserted and without help, unable to sense God's presence; he feels remote and separated from God, and is confused by various thoughts. We are clearly in second-mode territory: as he discerns, Ignatius is experiencing spiritual consolation and spiritual desolation.

Ignatius now must *discern the different spirits* at work in his spiritual consolations and desolations. When he experiences spiritual consolation, as in the first days described, he is consistently drawn toward one option in the choice he faces—the radical poverty he variously describes as "complete poverty," "perfect poverty," or more simply "no revenue." As the days pass, a pattern emerges: when Ignatius experiences *spiritual consolation* he is consistently drawn to *radical poverty*.

When, however, he experiences *spiritual desolation*, that drawing toward radical poverty is attacked. In the darkness, when Ignatius feels far from God and bereft of God's help, when his mind is filled with pain and confusion, the thought arises that he should "begin the Masses all over again." This thought says: "Earlier in this discernment you were convinced that you saw God's will clearly and that God wants the radical poverty. Look at you now. Nothing is clear. Everything is dark and confused. This discernment is ending badly. It has failed. You need to begin the forty days all over again." In the time of *spiritual desolation*, the clarity consistently given in spiritual consolation *is attacked*.

When Ignatius perceives this, his second-mode discernment is completed by the *experience of discernment of different spirits*. Since the *good spirit* counsels in time of *spiritual consolation* and since in spiritual consolation Ignatius is consistently drawn to radical poverty, he understands that God wills the radical poverty. Further, since in *spiritual desolation* this clarity is attacked and since in spiritual desolation the *enemy* counsels us, the attack in time of spiritual desolation on the clarity consistently given in time of spiritual consolation confirms all the more that God wills the radical poverty. Ignatius's second-mode discernment is complete, and in fact he concludes the discernment that day, sure that God wills the radical poverty.

The Official Directory describes this experience of discernment of different spirits in the following manner:

> In order, therefore, for a person to discover which of two alternatives on which he is deliberating is more pleasing to God, he should note in times of consolation to which side consolation and tranquility of soul incline him more; and on the contrary, when he experiences desolation, to which side that inclines him more. When he sees himself moved in opposite directions in these contrary times, he should take it as certain that the movements stem from contrary sources.[13]

Casanovas cites Ignatius's description of spiritual consolation in the *Spiritual Exercises* (*SpirEx*, 316) and adds the following:

> Whoever feels these most holy effects [of spiritual consolation] deeply and consistently in his soul whenever he considers choosing one option for God, and the opposite effects when he considers choosing the other option, may confidently take that substantial consolation as the voice of God who is calling him.[14]

This description of the spiritual consolation that renders second-mode discernment clear is worthy of note. Such consolation, Casanovas affirms, is *deep* and *consistent* when considering the one option. God gives rich spiritual consolation when the discerner considers the one option, and this consolation is consistent over time. Directors will watch for such deep and consistent spiritual consolation in judging whether or not God has given discerners second-mode clarity.

A look at concrete experiences will deepen our understanding of second-mode discernment and help to recognize it in practice.

Experiences of Second-Mode Discernment

We will examine four of these, each illustrating various nuances of second-mode discernment.

Richard's Story

Richard was discerning between marriage and Jesuit religious life.[15] In January of that year, he decided that God was calling him to marriage, yet was unable to find peace. He recounts the experience that resolved his struggle:

> The presence of sensible consolation when I reflected on joining the Jesuits was absolutely crucial for giving me the strength to make this decision. In retrospect it seems as though the Lord "tricked" me through this means to get past my own selfishness. Beginning in January of my senior year I began experiencing consolation during prayer in a way I never experienced before in my life. Indeed this was the beginning of my awakening to the Holy Spirit. I recall going up to church, sitting in front of the Sacred Heart altar and being absolutely overwhelmed. This was the first time I had ever experienced this type of enjoyment from being with God. And this consolation was present whenever I reflected seriously on the possibility of entering the Jesuits. If I began to lose this desire, I would simply return to my parish church, sit in front of the Sacred Heart altar, and again that consolation would be given me. Throughout this period I knew instinctively that this was the right decision for me because of this consolation. I had not the slightest knowledge of a technical process for finding God's will by reflecting on my inner experience nor did I have the help of a counselor. I simply had a confirmation of sensible consolation. . . .

Richard applied to the Jesuits in March and, seven months later, in August, entered the community. Of those seven months, he writes the following:

I recall that I experienced many doubts in my own decision to enter the Jesuits between the period of March to August. But whenever I went to the church and sat in silence, my experience of peace was restored and with it the conviction that God was calling me.[16]

The experience of consolation is evident in all Richard recounts. Directors will attend to note whether this is *spiritual* or *nonspiritual* consolation, and will hear the spiritual quality in Richard's description of his consolation: it is directly related to Jesus as the setting before the Sacred Heart altar indicates, and Richard knows that he experiences this joy and peace "from being with God." Richard clearly experiences spiritual consolation.

Directors will also note the *consistent pattern* of this spiritual consolation: repeatedly, over a period of time, "This consolation was present whenever I reflected seriously on the possibility of entering the Jesuits." In Richard's experience, the link between spiritual consolation and the choice to be a Jesuit is consistent. Directors, hearing Richard share this experience, will sense a second-mode discernment emerging. A point comes, in fact, when the pattern is so consistent that Richard gains "sufficient clarity and understanding"—all the clarity he needs—that God is calling him to be a Jesuit: "Throughout this period I knew instinctively that this was the right decision for me because of this consolation." When Richard relates this certitude, directors will recognize a second-mode discernment and confirm it.

Directors will note that Richard makes no mention of spiritual desolation and an attack on this certitude during it. If, after some gentle questioning, Richard has no more to say about spiritual desolation in his discernment, directors need insist no further. In second-mode discernment, spiritual consolation—what God is doing—is primary.[17] If, however, the enemy attempts to undermine God's work through spiritual desolation, discerners and their directors must note this well. Should, for example, Richard's clarity about the call to be a Jesuit be attacked in times of spiritual desolation, that desolation will serve as a further confirmation of his call to be a Jesuit.

Jessica's Story

When I met her, Jessica was in her eighties. As we spoke, she shared the story of the vocational discernment that led her into religious life. In a beautiful phrase, she called that discernment "a love affair." Such language immediately suggests the possibility of second-mode discernment in which God calls through an attraction of the heart.

Jessica tells of her discernment:

> I'm an organist and I see my life like a symphony. The opening theme was when I was in high school, sixteen or seventeen years old. There was an elusive kind of feeling, like a magnet drawing me. I loved being in church, the liturgy, the music. All of this drew me.
>
> Before high school I had thought of religious life, but not a lot. I just used to admire the sisters. But I didn't put too much thought into it. I dated. I had a couple of boyfriends, and I enjoyed life.
>
> One day during religion class, when I was a senior in high school, I looked out the window. I could see the cross on the top of the steeple of the parish church. I was drawn to that like a magnet drawing me.
>
> I went to daily Mass. There was something about Mass that drew me. I used to love to listen to the Scriptures. "Being drawn like a magnet" was a happy experience. There was a stillness about it. I used to like to look at the cross, listen to the music in church, all of this.

During our conversation, I asked Jessica if she could describe the happiness she felt in "being drawn like a magnet." Such deep places in the heart are not easy to describe, and Jessica simply answered,

> I entered into it. It was so elusive. I would watch the censor, the incense, the stained glass windows. I was just so involved in it. And I felt alone with it—I couldn't share it. I didn't think anyone would understand this. It was just being in this kind of atmosphere, being still, and enjoying it.

She continues:

> At times I would be at a dance and it would be fun, but I always felt that there was something more for me. And the "more" was God. As a junior in high school I was seriously thinking about religious life. By the time I was a senior, I knew. There wasn't one moment. It was a process, over time.
>
> I'd be at a dance or at a symphony or other social events, and I'd know there was more for me. I'd be happy with people, with friends. I'd be joyful, having a good time, but I'd feel like there was more for me, more that was drawing me. The "more" was God calling me to be his bride. When I told my parents they cried, and I said, I have to go. There was such a drawing, like a magnet draws.

Jessica thought of all she had shared, and concluded, "It's God's story with me. A love affair."

Jessica discerns between marriage and religious life. Over several years, her attraction toward religious life grows. Initially she is drawn to being in church and the liturgy but does not think seriously about religious life. Appropriately to her age, she dates and enjoys her social life. But the "magnet" continues to draw her: daily Mass, the cross, liturgical music, the stained glass windows, and the rest. Eventually Jessica understands that the drawing is toward a "more," and that for her the "more" is religious life: "By the time I was a senior, I knew." She adds, "There wasn't one moment. It was a process, over time."

Directors, when they hear this account, will sense the solidity of Jessica's certitude. They will note how it has matured over the years in a socially and religiously healthy setting. Certainly, Jessica discerns through an attraction of the heart. Is this second-mode discernment?

Directors will ask themselves: Is the drawing like a magnet an experience of *spiritual consolation*? Jessica's language in this regard is less explicit than Richard's. Directors will need to attend to her description of this drawing: "I used to *love* to listen to the Scriptures"; "'Being drawn like a magnet' was a *happy* experience"; "I used to *like* to look at the cross"; "It was just being in this kind of atmosphere, being still, and *enjoying* it." Jessica's language is certainly that of an uplift of heart, and the source of this uplift is clearly on the level of faith and her relationship with God. There appears little doubt that the drawing like a magnet is an experience of spiritual consolation. If so, we are in second-mode spiritual territory.

Directors will note too the *consistent pattern* over time: the uplift of heart, the spiritual consolation that Jessica experiences, *always* draws her toward involvement in the Church, an involvement that finally clarifies as a call to religious life: "The 'more' was God calling me to be his bride." A *consistent call to one option* in times of *spiritual consolation*: such is the nature of second-mode discernment. And Jessica receives "sufficient clarity and understanding" regarding her call through this discernment. As her account evidences, she is utterly certain that she has heard God's will. Directors, hearing what Jessica shares, will confirm the authenticity of her discernment.

Maria's Story

Maria is discerning between active and contemplative religious life.[18] She loves the active life of service and yet is beginning to feel drawn to cloistered religious life. She shares her experience:

> This desire came as something of a surprise to me. Yet, it also gave me joy and peace. I prayed a lot about it because I wasn't sure if this were from God or me. One thing I did notice was that when troubles arose inside or outside of me, this desire was not strong. Only when there was peace in my heart did the desire come back and stay with me. This happened several times. I spoke with my confessor about it, and he encouraged me to follow whatever God was asking.[19]

How should directors understand Maria's experience? Is this a second-mode discernment?

Maria feels a drawing toward cloistered religious life that gives her peace and joy. Directors will need to hear Maria describe further this peace and joy: Is it truly *spiritual* consolation? This may be true, but not enough is said in this brief account to be sure. And are the troubles Maria experiences interiorly *spiritual* desolation? Again, too little is said to be sure, and directors will need to hear Maria describe this further.

The attraction to cloistered life occurs "several times." Is this pattern clear enough to reveal second-mode discernment? This does not appear to be so. If we compare Maria's experience with the deep, repeated spiritual consolation that both Richard and Jessica feel toward one option in their discernment, directors will recognize that Maria is still in the early stages of this discernment, and that not enough data—not enough experiences of spiritual consolation and spiritual desolation—are present to judge that second-mode discernment has occurred. Maria may be experiencing the beginning of second-mode discernment, but may also be feeling an attraction of the moment that may not endure. Only time and further process will answer this question. At this point, Maria does not have "sufficient clarity and understanding," and any judgment would be premature. Maria and her director must, therefore, continue in the process.

One element promises well in the discernment: Maria's attentiveness to her spiritual experience. She is aware of the desires of her heart and can express them. She notes the experiences of peace and joy and also the times her heart is troubled. She perceives how the desire for cloistered life is present when her heart is at peace and how it weakens when her heart is troubled. She observes the patterns and can describe them to her guide. Maria is an excellent candidate for second-mode discernment in this regard. She images the awareness toward which directors must guide discerners who enter second-mode discernment.

Bruce's Story

When Bruce shared his story, at some points especially we were both deeply moved, Bruce even to tears. I include his story because it portrays the complexities that may be present in understanding the attractions of the heart. Such complexities, as Bruce's narrative shows, directly affect discernment of God's will, and directors must be aware of them.

Bruce begins his sharing:

> Before I entered the Franciscans, I was not looking to get married. I didn't feel that I could make it in marriage. I felt that I would botch it up, that I couldn't make anyone happy over a lifetime. I was afraid I would mess up the job. I dated a few

girls but wouldn't have thought of any of them as marriage-able. Marriage seemed like the default position, but it just didn't seem to fit for me.

I didn't really recognize the hole that was in my heart. My father was a World War II father who was never unfaithful and never hurt us, who worked hard to support his family, but just was distant. I loved God, and I loved the Church. That fills it up for a while, but as you spend time in prayer, things start to come to the surface.

I was with the Franciscans for almost three years, two years of postulancy and most of the novitiate. I was both happy and unhappy. I loved the Franciscans, and I learned how to pray and study. I loved the community. The moment I visited there, I knew I was supposed to be there. I had a deep certainty about that. But over time I began to feel unsettled, especially in the novitiate. I'd go walking in the neighborhood and see the lights in the homes, thinking: What's going on in there? I had a kind of longing that I couldn't fit into the happiness I felt in Franciscan life. But for me it had to be religious life or priesthood because that was the way I was going to please God. This was the best thing to do: it represented a full gift of self to God.

And there was a certain stubbornness in me. I wasn't going to be knocked off this. It was a decision I had made, really. I knew that many of the things I was doing were pleasing to God: community life, prayer, the study I was doing. All of these things were good. So what could possibly be wrong? Still, I always had this sense of uneasiness, of something not right. I thought this meant that maybe this wasn't the right order, that maybe I needed something else. I thought: maybe I'm not in right place, but this is what I'm supposed to do—be a religious or priest.

I longed for the hearth. That's why I was looking into those homes. They seemed so warm, and something in my heart wanted to be there. But I thought: this is what I have to deny myself.

Now events take an unexpected and painful turn for Bruce:

> So when the novice master told me, a month before first vows, that he would not recommend me for vows, I was completely shocked. I was stunned. Only later did I realize that he was seeing things in me that I wasn't seeing in myself. He had asked me to pray over things like my relationship with my father and even suggested that I try some counseling. I didn't want to do that because I didn't think there was any deep wound. He was trying to encourage freedom in me, freedom in the process of discernment.
>
> So I was stunned. I thought: I'm not entirely happy here, but things are good. These feelings, these desires for the hearth, to find out what was behind those doors, were temptations that I was resisting. And now this happens. What could possibly be going on?
>
> I walked out of his office, went outside, and looked up at the sky. It was a brilliant blue sky, and it spoke to me of Our Lady who had been so important in my spiritual journey. It told me that I was under her mantle. And I heard this in my heart: "I have something else for you." I took it to be Our Lady's voice. It set me free. I realized that the Franciscans had been good for me, but now I was supposed to go elsewhere.

Something new then enters Bruce's story and with it a struggle:

> I went home, worked for six months, and then went to graduate school. That was where I met Diane. From the moment I met her, I was head over heels in love with her. But it was a long, tortuous process because I knew she was thinking of religious life, and I was still thinking that I'd find a religious order somewhere, that I'd find a way to priesthood. And now I was in love with someone!
>
> I didn't tell anyone I was in love with her. She and I were moving around in these orbits trying to avoid each other. Neither of us wanted to interfere with God's plans or what we thought were God's plan. We spoke when we met and came to

know each other in social circumstances. Both of us struggled a lot. She was trying not to interfere with whatever was going on in me, and I was doing the same for her. And so we were both quietly wrestling the whole time.

I was still expressing interest in religious life and priesthood, and my spiritual director was trying to help me with this. He tried to help me dig my attraction for Diane out by the roots: It's a temptation. Just don't go there. But I couldn't make her go away. She was always there, and we were constantly running into each other. When I was trying to dig it out by the roots, I'd meet her coming out of a classroom or out of church. And it was all for naught! Every time I saw her I just fell in love with her again. I prayed. I made a retreat. Every time I'd commit myself to digging it out by the roots, I'd come back and meet her again, and I was in love again.

A key conversation now sheds light on the struggle:

Then I went to visit another religious order. While I was there, I spoke with one of the priests. I told him about my situation, how I kept trying to dig my love for Diane out by the roots, and it kept coming back. I told him that I was struggling along, sticking to my studies, that I hadn't said a word to her or anyone else, but that I just couldn't make it go away. He said: You know, you haven't asked God. You think you've already discerned it. You're not discerning it. You have to discern her. Then I realized that was the problem: once again I was deciding what direction I should go, and that I hadn't actually surrendered to God.

I talked to my spiritual director. I asked him: What about this? The priest suggested that I'm not discerning, that I'm just digging, that I'm just trying to root up something, that I'm not moving toward something. So I asked his permission, and he said, Yes, go ahead. I didn't do anything for a while, but I realized that I had to start opening up to matrimony as a possible state of life.

A new path now opens before Bruce:

Something changed in me just by being open to that. I had this love for Our Lady, but now I suddenly had an appreciation of the feminine that I hadn't had before. It was as though a part of the world opened up to me. It was a very vibrant experience. Suddenly I started to recognize what was behind those doors that I was longing to see behind when I was in novitiate. I started to appreciate the complementarity of male and female. I think I'd just been sort of suppressing all that. I started to feel freer in my prayer and finally was able to ask God: Is this what I'm supposed to be doing? Is this the direction I'm supposed to take?

I remember a breakthrough experience. Once again I was wrestling because I had this abiding feeling that it wouldn't be right for me to impose myself on someone else, that it would be a dirty trick to play on this nice young woman, that I couldn't possibly make her happy. That's what I really thought. One day I was upstairs in my apartment. I went into the basement, and I fell on my knees, and I asked God for her, and he gave her to me. And I actually saw her in her wedding dress. It was as though he had given her to me. It was very beautiful. That made me capable of finally broaching the subject of dating with her, of getting to know her.

Bruce's new freedom leads to openness with Diane:

Finally, on Easter Sunday, almost by accident, we ended up in a group in a park. We were all going for a walk. Diane and I ended up being separated from the group and walking alone. We just started speaking to each other, and it was a very odd conversation. I was trying to hint at things she didn't want to hear. I asked her if she was still thinking of the convent, and she said, no, I think I'd like to be married. I asked her: Are you taking applications? That made her very uncomfortable and she changed the subject. But the upshot was that she agreed to go out to dinner with me. Over time, I found that she had been thinking of me in the same way I'd been thinking of her for the last eight months, but hadn't wanted to give me any signs to derail me from seeking priesthood.

Then everything happened very quickly. Neither of us was interested in dating; we were just interested in each other. We were engaged in two weeks. Both of us were very sure, rock-solid sure. The remarkable thing was that in addition to coming awake to the beauty of the feminine, I recognized who I was. It was like a reintegration of myself. Who was I? Hers. I realized that I was for her. Everything that I was, that I was made to be, was ordered for this purpose. All of a sudden your prayer comes into line, and everything that God's been telling you for years just falls into place.

The biggest surprise for me was that my sexuality made sense in a way it never had before: Oh, this is what it's for. Because I'd learned to be chaste, but it was so hard, such a struggle. We were chaste before marriage, but all of that struggle went to rest, to peace. This is what you were made for, this is the person you were made for. All of a sudden that thing that is raucous and rambunctious finds its purpose, and it goes to rest. I felt like I had been reintegrated in this experience. But it was not easily won; it was a long journey.

Bruce's long discernment is sealed in marriage:

I have a photograph of a group of priests praying over me just before the wedding. It was a beautiful ceremony. We had a wonderful grace of confidence because God had just spoken so clearly. That's always been rock-solid. We've been married now for twenty-two years and have a beautiful family.

I mentioned that in college every time I saw Diane I just fell in love with her again. I still feel the same way today. It's a great gift. I tell her this all the time.

Again we are on holy ground, and we approach it with reverence. This is a story of increasing freedom to accept the desires that God has placed in a human heart.

Before he enters the Franciscans, Bruce never considers marriage possible for him: "I didn't feel that I could make it in marriage. I felt that I would botch it up, that I couldn't make anyone happy over a lifetime." Directors, like Bruce's novice master, will sense immediately that this must be explored. As Bruce says, at that time "I didn't really recognize the hole that was in my heart." What hole is this? How is this hole affecting Bruce's discernment? Directors will recognize that Bruce needs greater self-knowledge in this regard. They will invite him to pray and use the spiritual and human tools that can help him gain this knowledge.

   Though Bruce does not know of the hole in his heart, with great generosity he desires to give his life totally to God. This desire leads him to religious life: "For me it had to be religious life or priesthood because that was the way I was going to please God, this the best thing to do: it represented a full gift of self to God." And Bruce is firmly set in this decision: "There was a certain stubbornness in me. I wasn't going to be knocked off this. It was a decision I had made, really." Again, directors will sense that something is not sufficiently free in Bruce and will explore this with him.

   Though Bruce has made this decision, he experiences an uneasiness he cannot overcome: "But over time I began to feel unsettled. . . . I'd go walking in the neighborhood and see the lights in the homes, thinking: What's going on in there? I had a kind of longing that I couldn't fit into the happiness I felt in Franciscan life." Because he is so firmly set on religious life, Bruce can only see this longing as something God wishes him to renounce.

   Wisely, his novice master—an able spiritual guide in this—does not allow Bruce to take vows. The novice master senses that Bruce has good will and is generous, but is not free. An experience of prayer now gives Bruce the beginnings of that freedom: "I have something else for you."

   When Bruce meets Diane and falls in love the struggle escalates. Because he still pursues priesthood as the best way to give himself to God, he must "dig out by the roots" his love for Diane. Faithful to the counsel of his director, he tries to do this, but is unable. Bruce's experience alerts us to the disservice directors render discerners when they press discerners simply to suppress longings of the heart rather than discern them.[20]

   Bruce then meets a priest who understands the issue and helps Bruce to see it: "You haven't asked God. You think you've already discerned it. You're not discerning it. You have to discern her. Then I realized that was the problem: once again I was deciding what direction I should go, and that I hadn't actually surrendered to God." The priest, serving as a wise director in this, names the problem: *Bruce has not discerned.* With good will, Bruce believes that he has discerned and that God has called him to priesthood. But he has never discerned the longing for the hearth and the love for Diane he is experiencing. He has never felt free do so.

Now he gains this freedom, and true discernment begins: "Suddenly I started to recognize what was behind those doors that I was longing to see behind when I was in novitiate. I started to appreciate the complementarity of male and female. I think I'd just been sort of suppressing all that. I started to feel freer in my prayer and finally was able to ask God: Is this what I'm supposed to be doing? Is this the direction I'm supposed to take?" Bruce is no longer "suppressing all that," and discernment is now possible.

The rest occurs quickly. Bruce and Diane are now able to speak openly with each other and share the desire for marriage both feel. In the process, Bruce comes finally to understand his identity: "The remarkable thing was that in addition to coming awake to the beauty of the feminine, I recognized who I was. It was like a reintegration of myself. Who was I? Hers. I realized that I was for her. Everything that I was, that I was made to be, was ordered for this purpose. All of a sudden your prayer comes into line, and everything that God's been telling you for years just falls into place." *Everything that God's been telling you for years just falls into place:* Bruce is now able to recognize and accept the desires God has placed in his heart. Once he does this, his discernment is complete: "Both of us were very sure, rock-solid."

This is a discernment through an attraction of the heart, but it is not one of second-mode discernment. Bruce's long process of discernment is essentially *a journey toward freedom to accept an attraction inscribed into his heart*: "The vocation to marriage is written in the very nature of man and woman as they come from the hand of God."[21] Once Bruce is free to accept this calling as a real possibility in his life, he is integrated as a person and his discernment is clear: God is calling him to marriage and to marriage with Diane. Bruce has no need to pursue discernment further through Ignatius's modes.

I include Bruce's story in our discussion of second-mode discernment because it deals with an attraction of the heart and tells directors
that discernment according to such attractions is greatly hindered by
the lack of freedom to feel and accept them. To help Bruce, the director must recognize his lack of freedom and gently guide him beyond
it. At that point, as in Bruce's story, fruitful discernment is much more
likely to occur.

The examples given here—Richard's, Jessica's, Maria's, and
Bruce's experiences—indicate the importance of the director's role in
second-mode discernment. We turn now to that role.

Chapter Seven

An Attraction of the Heart
The Second Mode (II)

I call it consolation when some interior movement is caused in the soul, through which the soul comes to be inflamed with love of its Creator and Lord.

—St. Ignatius of Loyola

Having examined second-mode discernment in itself, we need now to explore the role of directors in such discernment. Much in second-mode discernment will depend on the directors' preparation and interaction with discerners. We will discuss *how directors should present* second-mode discernment to discerners, the *ways of doing* second-mode discernment they should provide discerners, and in what circumstances directors should judge that God has not given second-mode discernment and so should invite discerners *to move from second-mode to third-mode discernment.* In the final sections of this chapter, we will examine the role of the *second set of rules* for the discernment of spirits in second-mode discernment, and provide a *director's checklist* for such discernment.

Presenting Second-Mode Discernment

First-mode discernment, as a pure gift of God, does not require much explanation, and a brief presentation to discerners suffices. Second-mode discernment, however, because discerners must take an active role in it and because its central focus is the discernment of spirits, requires more explanation. The first mode, says Cordeses, should be explained "in passing"; the second must be explained "in detail."[1]

Teaching the Rules for Discernment

In presenting the second mode to discerners, "the first thing needed," writes González Dávila, "is an explanation of the nature of consolation and desolation as found in the first set of rules for the discernment of spirits."[2] We have already heard Ignatius tell directors that consolation "should be well explained," as should its contrary, desolation.[3]

Directors, therefore, before undertaking second-mode discernment with discerners must ask themselves: Do I know Ignatius's rules for the discernment of spirits (*SpirEx*, 313–36)? Do I know them well enough to teach them to discerners? To help discerners apply these rules to their experience? Sampaio writes: "The effectiveness of the second mode will grow as the director's knowledge and skill in the matter of discernment of spirits is greater. A purely speculative knowledge is not enough. Personal experience of the different spirits and how they work in the soul is of much greater importance."[4] Casanovas states that the director must guide second-mode discernment and adds that "this guidance will be more or less exact depending on how well he understands discernment of spirits."[5] As these authors indicate, the directors' knowledge of the two sets of rules must derive both from *study* of them and *personal experience* of them in their own lives.[6] Directors cannot help others apply these rules without learning them well and experiencing them in their own lives.

Applying the Rules for Discernment

In his preliminary annotations to the *Spiritual Exercises*, Ignatius provides a directory for the application of these rules (*SpirEx*, 6–10). These five annotations guide directors in applying the rules, and directors do well to assimilate them thoroughly. I provide a rapid summary of them here as an introduction to their content.

If discerners do not experience spiritual consolation or desolation, directors are to verify that they are faithfully using the spiritual means for discernment: daily prayer with Scripture, review of their prayer, the examen prayer, and the other means (*SpirEx*, 6). Should discerners be burdened by spiritual desolation and temptations, directors are not to be harsh with them but gentle and encouraging, helping them to understand the tactics of the enemy and disposing them to receive future consolation (*SpirEx*, 7).

Directors are to explain the two sets of rules according to the needs of discerners (*SpirEx*, 8–10): if they are tempted openly and obviously ("Should you say yes to God's call, it will be difficult, cost you much sacrifice, others will esteem you less," and the like), the first set of rules; if they are generous with God and may be tempted more subtly under the appearance of good (a pastor is drawn to leave his fruitful parish ministry and enter a monastery in order to dedicate himself more deeply to prayer), the second set of rules. The ability to distinguish which of these two tactics the enemy may be employing with discerners and to apply opportunely the appropriate set of rules to their experience is one of the most necessary skills for directors who accompany others' discernments.[7] As we have said earlier, prayer, study, and experience are required to attain this skill.

Fostering Spiritual Awareness

Throughout second-mode discernment, directors must encourage discerners to pray with the life of Jesus in the Gospels. Discerners do this to draw near to Jesus, seeking interior knowledge of him in order to love him more and follow him more closely (*SpirEx*, 104)—that is, so that they will grow more apt to find God's will in the choice at hand. Ideally this prayer should be daily and of an hour's duration or close to it, not less than a half-hour. It should conclude with the review we have discussed above. These times of prayer, the Official Directory states, "strengthen and illuminate the mind, lifting it from earthly things and making it more fit to perceive and embrace God's will and to overcome all obstacles."[8] Such prayer assists discerners because second-mode discernment "presumes a union and harmony of perspective between the person and God; it presupposes in the person an interior and connatural knowledge of the thought and heart of Jesus."[9] Such union and knowledge are best fostered by daily prayer of this kind. To cease from such prayer during second-mode discernment "would weaken and becloud the soul";[10] without this prayer, second-mode discernment loses its heart.

God works in discerners' hearts not only during formal prayer but also throughout the day. Second-mode discernment progresses more

surely when discerners note any spiritual consolations and desolations, with their related attractions and resistances, they may experience during the day.[11] Outside the times of prayer, writes Polanco, the
discerner "should continue mulling this matter over and watching in
the same way for the above-mentioned movements."[12] When discernment occurs in daily life, discerners will do this primarily through
the examen prayer.[13] Directors must teach discerners this prayer and
invite them to pray it faithfully for some ten to fifteen minutes a
day. If discerners do both—pray daily with Jesus in the Gospels and
review their prayer, and also pray the daily examen—they are likely
to grasp the spiritual movements on which second-mode discernment
is based.[14]

The Official Directory affirms that the discerner "should be told
to put down briefly in writing the principal consolations and lights,
as well as his good desires and resolutions."[15] The same counsel obviously applies also to spiritual desolations and to the thoughts and
desires that arise during them. If this counsel is wise within the days
of the Exercises, it is more so outside the retreat when the process
may require several months and must occur within the busyness of
daily activity. Without written reviews of daily prayer and of the daily
examen, discerners are unlikely to grasp the patterns that permit "sufficient clarity and understanding" in second-mode discernment. In
practice, discerners must keep a journal, should review it before their
meetings with their directors, and generally should bring it to the
meetings as an aid to sharing the spiritual movements experienced
since the last meeting. Their directors must invite them to keep this
journal and explain the reasons for it.[16]

The meeting should be monthly at least, and very likely more fre-
quent when the process of discernment reaches its heart. Directors
should allot an hour for the meeting, even though discerners may not
always need the entire hour. As they move toward the heart of the
discernment, discerners are more likely to require the full hour: in
second-mode discernment there is much to share.

After a brief welcome, directors will generally begin the meeting
with a prayer.[17] Their first task then is to listen as discerners describe
the spiritual consolations and desolations, with their related attractions and resistances, experienced since the last meeting—the spiri-

tual movements they have noted in the review of their daily prayer and their daily examen. When directors sense that points of importance have been touched, they will invite discerners to describe these more fully. As needed, directors will apply the rules for the discernment of spirits to help discerners understand their spiritual experience. Based on the discerners' experiences, their directors will offer suggestions for prayer until the next meeting. Directors may invite discerners to repeat certain texts that have had special resonance for them (*SpirEx*, 118) and may propose others that they judge helpful in light of what discerners have shared. As the meeting concludes, directors will encourage the discerners and hearten them to continue the process.

One directory invites directors to reflect after the meeting on what discerners have shared: "The director should carefully observe and later reflect on what the person has told him about the progress and goal of his meditations so as to learn the movements of the good angel, the good desires, holy inspirations, and spiritual consolations that the person experienced; and, on the other hand, the temptations, maneuvers, and wiles of the demon, the dejection of soul, etc., so that perceiving these clearly, he can better guide himself and the person, and provide opportune help as necessary."[18]

Ways of Doing Second-Mode Discernment

When discerners are prepared to undertake second-mode discernment, how will they proceed in practice? What process should directors present to them for engaging in second-mode discernment? The commentators outline three possible ways of doing second-mode discernment.[19] Directors may present one or more of these to discerners as the directors judge most helpful for individual discerners. To render these three ways more concrete, we will apply each to Richard's discernment between Jesuit priesthood and marriage (Chapter 6).

Simply Observe What Happens

As always, we presuppose that discerners are praying daily with the Gospel and also praying the examen prayer. In a first way of doing second-mode discernment, directors simply invite discerners to note any movements of spiritual consolation or desolation they may experience as they pray, and to identify the thoughts, desires, attractions, or resistances with regard to the options they face, that may arise during these movements. They ask discerners to do this day after day, week after week, during second-mode discernment. Directors and discerners together watch to see if a clear pattern occurs: a consistent attraction toward one option in times of spiritual consolation, and any attack on that attraction they may experience when in spiritual desolation. Should such a pattern emerge consistently and clearly over enough time, directors will confirm for discerners that "sufficient clarity and understanding" (*SpirEx*, 176) have been reached. If such a pattern does not emerge clearly, directors will judge that God is not calling these discerners to second-mode discernment and will invite them to begin third-mode discernment.

In Richard's case, for example, his director will watch to see the thoughts and attractions that arise when Richard experiences spiritual consolation. As the weeks and months pass, Richard and his director will note that whenever Richard experiences spiritual consolation, he is consistently drawn to be a Jesuit. When this pattern repeats over time until it is firmly established, they know that God has called Richard to be a Jesuit through second-mode discernment. Should Richard's clarity be attacked in time of spiritual desolation, he and his director will see in that attack a further confirmation of his call to be a Jesuit.

If, however, Richard feels drawn to be a Jesuit at times when he experiences spiritual consolation, but does not always feel this drawing when in spiritual consolation, or even feels a drawing toward marriage in other times of spiritual consolation, then "sufficient clarity and understanding" have not been reached in second-mode discernment. The same may be said if Richard has few experiences of spiritual consolation and desolation, too few to permit a clear pattern to emerge. In these cases, the director will not immediately move Richard to third-mode discernment but will allow further time to see if experiences of spiritual consolation and desolation may be given. When enough time and trial have been made and if sufficient clarity still has not emerged, then the director will invite Richard to begin third-mode discernment.

Present Both Options to God

In this way of doing second-mode discernment, directors invite discerners to seek second-mode discernment more actively. They instruct discerners to note when they experience spiritual consolation and, during those times, to present to God the one and the other alternative. Discerners are to present these options to God without inclining their hearts toward the one or the other. In a time of spiritual consolation, for example, Richard will first present to God the vocation of Jesuit priesthood and then the vocation to marriage, and will do so without inclining his heart to either, simply presenting both to God. When discerners present these options to God, they watch to see toward which the consolation inclines more: toward which they experience more spiritual peace, energy, encouragement, desire, and joy, that is, toward which they experience more strongly the effects of spiritual consolation (*SpirEx*, 316). Directors also instruct discerners to present both options in times of spiritual desolation and to note toward which they experience more the effects of the desolation: disquiet of heart, diminishment of energy, discouragement, and sadness (*SpirEx*, 317).

Discerners are to do this often when they experience spiritual consolation and desolation. They are to reflect on these experiences in their reviews of prayer and in their examen prayer. Discerners may note that a pattern emerges, that in spiritual consolation the effects of the consolation are consistently stronger when they present one option to God rather than the other. If so, they will continue to present the two options to God in spiritual consolation until they have "sufficient clarity and understanding" and their directors judge that God has given them second-mode discernment. If that clarity is consistently attacked by more notable effects of spiritual desolation when they present that same option in time of desolation, then that clarity will be further confirmed. If, however, a pattern does not emerge or begins to emerge but is not consistently confirmed, then directors will judge that God has not given second-mode discernment and will invite discerners to begin the third mode.

If Richard, for example, in times of spiritual consolation, presents both Jesuit life and marriage to God, and consistently finds the effects of the consolation stronger when he presents Jesuit life, he and his director will recognize that God may be giving Richard second-mode discernment. If this pattern repeats clearly over enough time, the director will judge that God has in fact given Richard second-mode discernment. Should the effects of spiritual desolation be stronger whenever Richard presents Jesuit life, this clarity will be further confirmed.

Richard, however, may also present Jesuit life and marriage when in spiritual consolation and find that no clear pattern emerges. Richard may, for example, sometimes feel stronger effects of spiritual consolation when he considers Jesuit life and at other times when he considers marriage. Likewise, no clear pattern of stronger effects in time of spiritual desolation may emerge. Richard may also experience too few times of spiritual consolation and desolation for any pattern to appear. Unless this should change and a clear pattern emerge, Richard's director will judge that God is not giving him second-mode discernment and will invite him to begin third-mode discernment.

Present Both Options to God as if Already Chosen

In a final way of doing second-mode discernment, directors instruct discerners to present first one and then the other option to God, but now—by contrast with the preceding way—as if they have already chosen that option. They present the first option to God on one day, speaking to God about it, offering this option to God, and asking that he choose them for it. On another day they do the same for the other option, and on subsequent days or weeks, according to the time their directors judge opportune, continue to repeat this alternation.

Thus on one day, Richard presents Jesuit life to God as if he had already chosen it. He offers the choice of Jesuit life to God, asking that this be God's will and that God call him to live Jesuit life. On the next day, Richard does the same with marriage, presenting it to God as if he had already chosen it. He offers the call to marriage to God, asking that this be God's will and that God call him to live married life. Richard continues this alternation a number of times in his prayer.

In the preceding way of doing second-mode discernment, discerners wait until they experience spiritual consolation or desolation to present the one option and then the other to God. In this, they may present the options at any time, alternating the one with the other in successive times of prayer.

As they do this, discerners watch to see toward which option God gives greater signs of his preference. Does God appear to give greater grace and spiritual consolation when one option is presented? Is there a consistent pattern of this over time? If so, God may be giving second-mode discernment to the discerners.[20] As with the other ways of doing second-mode discernment, if no pattern emerges or if directors judge that the pattern has not emerged clearly enough, they will conclude that God has not given second-mode discernment and will invite the discerners to begin third-mode discernment.

Thus if Richard consistently experiences greater grace and spiritual consolation when he presents Jesuit priesthood to God, offering this option to God and asking that God chose him for it, and if this pattern repeats over time such that sufficient clarity and understanding are reached, he and his director will judge that God has given Richard second-mode discernment and that God is calling Richard to Jesuit priesthood. On the other hand, should Richard experience greater grace and spiritual consolation when he presents marriage to God, offering this option to God and asking that God choose him for it, and if this pattern repeats over time such that sufficient clarity and understanding are reached, then he and his director will judge that God has given Richard second-mode discernment, and that God is calling Richard to marriage. But if no pattern emerges or at least not with sufficient clarity, then the director will judge that God has not given Richard second-mode discernment and will counsel him to begin third-mode discernment.

Such are the three ways in which directors may invite discerners to undertake second-mode discernment. Directors may present one or more of these ways when they instruct discerners on how to proceed in second-mode discernment. Which of these three ways or which combination of them directors propose to discerners will depend on what directors judge will best aid individual discerners.

A final consideration regards when discerners should apply these ways of doing second-mode discernment. The commentators suggest various possibilities. The Official Directory affirms that these ways may be employed at the end of each time of prayer or "in any time during the prayer when the soul is tranquil."[21] Polanco suggests that time dedicated to second-mode discernment be interspersed with meditation such that, on some days, discerners meditate on Jesus in the Gospels and on others devote time to second-mode discernment.[22] The Official Directory further counsels that the discerner "should do the same thing outside the time of meditation, setting the matter before himself as described above and watching to observe the movements."[23] Thus his director may suggest to Richard that he present Jesuit life and marriage to God during his daily time of prayer when his heart is at peace, or regularly at the end of his prayer, or that on some days he dedicate entire times of prayer to this, or that he do so outside the time of prayer when he is free. Directors will adapt these suggestions to the needs of individual discerners.

When Is It Time to Move to Third-Mode Discernment?

When should directors judge that God has not given second-mode discernment and that they should invite discerners to begin third-mode discernment? Polanco writes that this should be done if discerners experience no notable consolations or desolations, or if they experience such movements toward both options.[24] Cordeses affirms that if discerners experience no significant movements or if they are unsure that those they did experience were from God, they should move to the third mode.[25] González Dávila adds that when discerners do not feel "full peace and satisfaction" with their second-mode discernment, they should move to the third mode.[26] Thus if either of the two experiences (SpirEx, 176) that permit second-mode discernment is lacking—either there were not enough consolations and desolations (first experience) or the discernment of these experiences was not sufficiently clear (second experience)—directors must move discerners to third-mode discernment.

Hernández counsels that this not be done lightly: "In this case, St. Ignatius desires that we *not move immediately* to the third mode, but that we persist before God in seeking the clarity we need in discerning the movements the person has experienced, in asking for and awaiting such movements, in begging of God clearer signs of whether or not he desires the option toward which the lights and movements appear to tend. . . . If, notwithstanding these efforts, such lights and movements are not given, we should then have recourse to the third mode."[27]

The Second Set of Rules for the Discernment of Spirits

Thus far we have explored second-mode discernment in the context of the *first set of rules* for the discernment of spirits (*SpirEx*, 313–27). In the experience that these fourteen rules describe, the *good spirit* works through the joy of *spiritual consolation* and the *enemy* through the discouragement of *spiritual desolation*. In fact, when Ignatius describes second-mode discernment he does so as an "experience of *consolations* and *desolations*" (*SpirEx*, 176).[28]

Thus, when Ignatius discerns between radical and mitigated poverty, he finds that in time of *spiritual consolation* he is consistently drawn to radical poverty, whereas in time of *spiritual desolation* that drawing is attacked. Both the drawing in spiritual consolation (action of the good spirit) and the attack on that drawing in spiritual desolation (action of the enemy) confirm that God wills the radical poverty. Such is second-mode discernment according to the first set of rules.

The directories repeatedly remind directors, however, that the *second set of rules* is of great importance in second-mode discernment.[29] Second-mode discernment according to the second set of rules is the most refined discernment directors may encounter in adopting Ignatius's three modes. Once more, therefore, we repeat: directors must know these rules well if they are to guide discerners responsibly in such discernment. A word about the second set of rules and a concrete example will clarify the directors' task.

The Second Set of Rules

Earlier I provided a rapid summary of these eight rules, and elsewhere I have discussed them in detail.[30] Here I can give only a brief review with the director's role specifically in mind.

In the two sets of rules, Ignatius describes two different spiritual situations and how the good spirit and enemy act in both. The *first spiritual situation* is described in the *first set of rules* (*SpirEx*, 313–27). In it the *good spirit* works through *spiritual consolation* (in the joy of spiritual consolation, Ignatius is drawn to radical poverty), and the *enemy* works through its contrary, that is, through *spiritual desolation* (in the discouragement of spiritual desolation, Ignatius's drawing to radical poverty is attacked).

In the *second spiritual situation* described in the *second set of rules* (*SpirEx*, 328–36), the *good spirit* continues to work through *spiritual consolation*. Now, however, the *enemy* changes tactics and imitates the working of the good spirit, *also giving spiritual consolation* with a drawing toward a good and holy thing, but *a different good and holy thing* than what God wills for the person. Thus, for example, the pastor may experience joyful spiritual consolation in the thought of leaving his fruitful ministry in the suburban parish and requesting an inner-city parish in order to imitate Jesus more closely in his service to the poor. In this second spiritual situation, that spiritual consolation is no longer a sure sign of the good spirit. Because the good spirit and the enemy now both use the *same tactic*—both give the joy of spiritual consolation with a drawing toward a good and holy thing—the discernment is more refined than in the first spiritual situation in which the good spirit and enemy use *contrary tactics*, that is, when the good spirit gives the joy of *spiritual consolation* and the enemy the discouragement of *spiritual desolation*.

Ignatius tells directors that the enemy employs the more basic tactic of spiritual desolation when discerners' lives of faith are as yet on a basic level. These persons sincerely love God and genuinely desire to do his will, but may fear the cost of accepting God's will, be discouraged in considering what they must renounce to do that will, be disheartened at what others may say, and so forth (*SpirEx*, 9). In such, the enemy employs the tactic of spiritual desolation (first spiritual situation) to discourage them and dissuade them from doing God's will.[31]

When discerners have grown more in the love of God, have become more generous with God, and more desirous of dedicating their lives to his service, they are less likely to succumb to spiritual desolation. Consequently, Ignatius affirms, the enemy shifts his tactics and imitates the good spirit, *giving deceptive spiritual consolation* with a drawing toward a good thing other than that which God wills (second spiritual situation: *SpirEx*, 10). Directors need, therefore, to note well at what stage of the spiritual journey discerners find themselves in order to identify which of these two tactics the enemy may use.

In this more refined second spiritual situation, how can we discern between experiences of joyful spiritual consolation that draw discerners toward different options? How can directors help them in such sensitive discernment?

In the second set of rules, Ignatius gives his answer. He asks directors above all *to watch the unfolding of the drawing.* The enemy, he says, can imitate the good spirit *in the beginning*, giving joyful spiritual consolation and a drawing toward a good and holy thing.[32] But as the drawing toward this good and holy thing unfolds (the *middle*) and leads toward a conclusion (the *end*), if the enemy is at work, a diminishment will inevitably emerge: directors will note that the choice toward which discerners now incline is less objectively good than what they had planned before, or that as discerners focus on this choice their spiritual energy weakens or they grow more troubled. If the good spirit is at work in the spiritual consolation and drawing toward the good and holy thing, none of this diminishment will occur (*SpirEx*, 333).[33]

If, for example, Richard is a generous person of this kind and experiences joyful spiritual consolation not only at the thought of Jesuit life but more recently also at the thought of marriage, his director will watch to see if any diminishment occurs as this new drawing unfolds: Does this new drawing begin, even though in spiritual consolation, with a subtle sense of trouble (like water on a rock: *SpirEx*, 335)? As Richard continues to consider this new drawing, does he grow less generous with the Lord or more troubled in heart (*SpirEx*, 333–34)? Directors, with the second set of rules in mind, will watch for such signs: these are the key to accurate second-mode discernment according to the second set of rules. An example will render such discernment more concrete.

Patricia's Story

In her earlier years, Patricia never thought much about God. Twenty years ago, however, when she was in college, the experience of a difficult time showed Patricia how much she needed God and moved her to embrace her faith as a personal commitment. Since that time, she pursued her new life of faith with courage and dedication. She involved herself actively in the chapel community, began to pray daily, participated in student retreats, and spoke regularly with the chaplain. Patricia's life acquired new meaning through her growing faith, and God's love became increasingly real for her. Her deepening faith also awakened a desire to serve others, and Patricia assisted in various initiatives of service to the poor. The sense of purpose and the joy evident in her life began to draw others, and Patricia became a quiet but effective apostle for the Lord.

One year after college, Patricia married a man who shared her life of faith, and they had three children. Through the years, Patricia continued to pray daily and to be active in her parish, above all in service to the poor; as previously in college, she encountered Christ in a special way through assisting the disadvantaged. When Patricia would return to her family after some hours of this service, she would find her faith stronger and her awareness of Christ in her husband and children more alive.

Recently her pastor, aware of Patricia's love for the poor and knowing that her children were now in college, asked Patricia to consider creating a program of service to the poor in the parish. The need was real, and the program would provide an opportunity to help many. As Patricia and the pastor spoke about this, she realized that heading the program would be demanding. It would require most of her free time and the sacrifice of other activities she had hoped to undertake. It would also mean that she and her husband would have to relinquish their thoughts of moving. The pastor invited Patricia to take all the time she needed to decide.

Patricia spoke with her husband and found that he was open to the pastor's suggestion. She also spoke with her spiritual director, who suggested that she pray about the decision for some weeks and that she review her prayer and pray the examen daily. The director agreed to meet with Patricia regularly during those weeks.

When Patricia prayed about the program for the poor, she consistently felt joyful and close to the Lord, with a drawing toward this service. As the weeks unfolded, Patricia found her heart strongly inclined to say yes to the pastor. After sharing this with her director in their most recent meeting, Patricia felt that the discernment was nearing completion.

The next Sunday, Patricia attended Mass with her husband and children. The Gospel spoke of Christ's presence in those in need (Matt 25:31–46), and Patricia was especially struck by the words "I was . . . a stranger and you welcomed me" (Matt 25:35). Earlier that week she had learned that in a few months her city would receive refugees from a war-torn third-world country, and that volunteers to assist them would be urgently needed. When she heard the priest proclaim Jesus' words "I was . . . a stranger and you welcomed me," Patricia felt the Lord's presence, and spiritual joy filled her heart. She sensed that the Lord was addressing those words to her personally and in the context of the refugees. The thought of welcoming Christ in the impoverished refugees gave joy to her heart, and desire for this service grew warm within her.

Patricia recognized, however, that she could not both begin the program in the parish and serve the refugees. Finding that her heart experienced joy and a drawing toward both projects, and recognizing that both were good, Patricia was confused. She only wanted to do God's will, but now did not know how to find it. Unsure of how to discern, Patricia spoke with her director and asked for help.[34]

How will the director respond to Patricia's request? What should directors do in similar situations? Was Patricia's growing conviction that God was calling her to lead the parish program an accurate discernment of God's will? What then should be said of the spiritual joy and drawing toward the new project—the service of the refugees—clearly also a valuable ministry? Does this joy and drawing signify that God wills her to serve the refugees rather than direct the parish program?

Directors will first note that Patricia may be the generous person Ignatius intends in the second set of rules: for years she has lived her faith deeply, prayed faithfully, and grown in loving service of her family, her parish, and the poor. Aware of this, directors will remember the *second set of rules* and the possibility that *the enemy* may bring Patricia joyful *spiritual consolation* with a drawing toward *a good thing that God does not want for her*, and that will ultimately lead to diminishment in Patricia's spiritual life and service of others. In fact, Patricia is now experiencing spiritual consolation toward two different good options. If the enemy is at work, he is no longer working through *spiritual desolation* as in the first spiritual situation and first set of rules, but rather through *spiritual consolation*—the tactic of the enemy Ignatius highlights in the second set of rules. The enemy may be attempting to deceive Patricia, as Ignatius says, disguised as an angel of light (*SpirEx*, 332).

Because the enemy may now be working through spiritual consolation, directors know they must watch the *beginning, middle,* and *end* of this new drawing in Patricia (Second Rules, rules 3 through 7: *SpirEx*, 331–35).[35] As Patricia recounts the experience of that Sunday, directors will look to see if, together with the joyful spiritual consolation, Patricia expresses any sense of even subtle disturbance in that experience. This is to ask, in Ignatian terms, whether this new drawing *began* like *water on a rock* or *water entering a sponge* (*SpirEx*, 335). If the former, directors have a first indication that this new drawing may not be of God.

Directors will also attend to the *middle* and *end* of this drawing in Patricia, that is, as the weeks unfold and Patricia shares her reviews of prayer and her daily examen, do directors note any *diminishment* in Patricia's peace of heart (subjective diminishment) or plans to serve the Lord (objective diminishment) (*SpirEx*, 334)?[36] Again, if so, directors will have further indications that the enemy was at work in the spiritual consolation and drawing toward serving the refugees of that Sunday morning. If directors do note such diminishment, they and Patricia will seek to identify the steps that led little by little to this diminishment (*SpirEx*, 334) in order to avoid similar tactics of the enemy in the future.

Should directors note no such diminishment in Patricia—she remains at peace and joyful in the Lord as the weeks progress, and her plans to serve the Lord remain as strong as before that Sunday morning—then they and Patricia will need to consider the real possibility that God may wish the service of the refugees. Ignatius writes: "If the beginning, middle, and end is all good, inclined to all good, it is a sign of the good angel" (*SpirEx*, 333).

The same approach would apply to the case cited earlier of the pastor whose ministry greatly blesses and heals a divided suburban parish, working great good for many, and who in a time of spiritual consolation feels drawn to request an inner-city parish in order to serve the poor more directly as Jesus himself did. When this pastor asks his director's help to discern whether God wants him to remain in his suburban parish or request the inner-city parish, how will his director assist him? Here too the director will note the *beginning*, *middle*, and *end*: Did the new thought first come to the pastor like water on a rock or like water entering a sponge? Is there any diminishment of this man's availability to serve or interior peace as the weeks of discernment unfold? Ignatius counsels this approach to directors whenever generous persons are drawn in time of spiritual consolation toward different good options in their discernment.[37]

A Note on Second-Mode Clarity

Various commentators note that second-mode discernment based on experiences of spiritual consolation and desolation, if it is authentic, must concord with the light that God gives through other means as well. Casanovas writes: "Although divine movements are the characteristic of this second mode, this in no way signifies that reason and the other means of which we dispose to know the truth are excluded. These movements must be examined by the rules for the discernment of spirits to see if they are of God, and in those rules are found all the sure criteria we possess to know the truth, above all in divine things."[38]

González Dávila affirms that interior movements must be tested by "light," and "This light is the word of God, the Church and the public magisterium of God in the Church, together with human reason; all these are from God and cannot be mutually contradictory."[39] Thus, any presumed second-mode discernment based on discerners' experiences of spiritual consolation and desolation that would contradict the Scriptures, the teaching of the Church, or human reason, could not be considered genuine.

Directors do well to note any such contradictions should they surface. If they do, the directors will advise their directees that "sufficient clarity and understanding" (*SpirEx*, 176) have not been given—or at least not yet been given—through second-mode discernment. The process must continue.[40]

Second-Mode Discernment: A Director's Checklist

When directors assist discerners in judging whether God has given them second-mode discernment, the following questions will assist them:

- Has this person *experienced spiritual consolation and spiritual desolation* during this process of discernment?
- Are these consolations and desolations *truly spiritual*—on the level of faith and the person's relationship with God?[41]
- Has the person *been attentive* to these experiences of spiritual consolation and desolation? Has the person noted these in the review of daily prayer and in the examen prayer? Has the person kept a journal of these experiences?
- Has the person *shared* these with the director so that the director may accompany insightfully the discernment?
- Does the director see a *clear pattern of attraction in spiritual consolation* toward one option in the choice?
- Has this pattern been attacked in times of *spiritual desolation*?
- Has the pattern repeated enough times to give *sufficient clarity and understanding*? Does the director judge that second-mode discernment is complete and clear?

- Or are there *too few experiences* of spiritual consolation and desolation to reach sufficient clarity? Are there *contrasting attractions* in time of spiritual consolation so that no pattern emerges clearly?
- Does the director judge that second-mode clarity has not been given sufficiently and that it is time to invite the person *to third-mode discernment*?

Chapter Eight

A Preponderance of Reasons
The Third Mode (I)

Better than anyone else, the Holy Spirit will teach you how to taste with the heart and carry out with sweetness what reason shows to be for the greater service and glory of God.
— St. Ignatius of Loyola

When discerners have not found God's will through interior movements—when God has not given sufficient clarity and understanding through the experience of spiritual consolations and desolations that characterizes the second mode—then, Ignatius says, they should employ their own *natural powers* to seek God's will (*SpirEx*, 177–88).[1] In the context Ignatius will carefully describe, they employ their reason, enlightened by faith and open to God's grace, to discern his will. In this way, Casanovas writes, Ignatius "admirably combines our action with that of God."[2] As a result, Polanco adds, "the one discerning can answer fully to God for the choice he has made since he has done all in his power to learn God's will when he was unsure of having found it in the second mode."[3] This use of our natural powers to seek God's will constitutes, Ignatius tells us, a third mode of discernment.

Third-Mode Discernment: What Is It?

In the preceding chapter, we accompanied Ignatius through a discernment regarding radical or mitigated poverty. As we saw, during those days Ignatius attentively noted experiences of spiritual consolation and spiritual desolation—he discerned according to the second mode. But while Ignatius discerned according to such interior movements, he did something else as well—he prayerfully reviewed the *concrete factors* in this discernment: What advantages and what disadvantages would follow if he and his companions adopted a mitigated poverty? A more radical poverty? Ignatius also asked: Do these concrete factors *reveal God's will* in this discernment? Clearly, in doing this Ignatius adopted a further mode of discernment, one no longer based on experiences of consolation and desolation (second mode), but on consideration of the advantages and disadvantages of either option—he adopted a third mode of discernment.[4]

Ignatius identified various *advantages* to *mitigated poverty*: the Society of Jesus would be better maintained; its members would not trouble others by begging; they would be less exposed to disordered concern for their material welfare; the time necessary for begging would be free for preaching, confessions, and other works of ministry; their churches would be better maintained and so foster greater devotion, and so forth. Ignatius found eight such advantages for mitigated poverty.[5]

But Ignatius also perceived *disadvantages* to this *mitigated poverty*: the members would be less diligent in helping others, less ready to go on journeys and endure hardships, and less able to draw others to true poverty.

When, however, Ignatius considered the *advantages* of *radical poverty*, the list grew long: the members would have greater spiritual strength and greater devotion through imitation of Jesus, who lived in such poverty; they would overcome worldly avarice more easily; their hearts would be more united through sharing the same complete poverty; they would more readily hope for everything from God; they would live more humbly and more united with their humble Lord; they would be less inclined to desire worldly consolation; they would give greater witness as others saw that they did not desire worldly things—the list extended to seventeen reasons.[6] Ignatius considered that the *disadvantages* of *radical poverty* coincided with the advantages of mitigated poverty already outlined, and did not repeat them. When Ignatius reviewed this list of advantages and disadvantages, the result was clear to him: a preponderance of reasons favored the choice for radical poverty.

As is evident, this mode of discernment reviews the *reasons* that support one or the other option, and attempts to identify toward which a preponderance of reasons inclines. As Ignatius's reasons further reveal, these are reasons based on faith and on the greater service of God. In Ignatius's vocabulary, these reasons suggest that the option considered will serve *God's greater glory*, that is, that this option will serve to make God more known and loved in human hearts in this life and for eternity. A glance at Ignatius's reasons as listed here reveals this single focus on God's greater glory—on what will make God more known and loved—in every reason Ignatius cites: greater spiritual strength in the members, greater hope in God, greater unity with their humble Lord, more effective witness, and the like in each reason named.

When, Ignatius says, God has not shown his will by the first mode of discernment (clarity beyond doubting), and when sufficient clarity and understanding have not been given through the second (experience of consolations and desolations), we proceed to this *third mode* of discernment.[7] We turn now to his text in the *Spiritual Exercises*.

A Time of Tranquility

Third-mode discernment requires, Ignatius tells us, a "tranquil" time (*SpirEx*, 177). He explains: "I said a tranquil time, that is, when the soul is not agitated by different spirits and uses its natural powers freely and tranquilly" (*SpirEx*, 177). When, therefore, directors consider inviting discerners to this third mode, they must carefully ascertain whether or not the discerners are in this *tranquil time*.

The tranquil time is present, Ignatius writes, "when the soul is not agitated by different spirits." Discerners, consequently, must not be troubled by the *spiritual desolations* and *temptations* of the enemy. A certain level of *spiritual consolation* may actually assist third-mode discernment, but must not be so intense that discerners are "agitated" and therefore less apt to reason well.[8]

At the same time, discerners must not be agitated on the *non-spiritual* (physical and psychological) level to such a degree that they cannot reason well. Directors must note any "worry, preoccupying concerns, fatigue, distracting surroundings, anguish, anger, or any highly exciting emotions of delight, joy, and so on"[9] or any illness[10] that might impede clear reasoning. Should these be present and for as long as they persist, directors must not invite discerners to third-mode discernment.

This tranquil time, Ignatius continues, permits discerners to use their *natural powers* freely and tranquilly. By "natural powers" Ignatius intends "those powers used in the third mode of discerning God's will: insight, reason, imagination, memory, and will."[11] Third-mode discernment requires that discerners be *tranquil* in order to use these *natural powers* well: so that they may think clearly, see well the advantages and disadvantages for God's greater glory of the one option and the other, grasp accurately the weight of each, and judge rightly which option better serves God's glory—which option will make God more known and loved in human hearts. Directors must judge whether or not discerners are able to use their natural powers in this way. If so, the discerners may undertake third-mode discernment.

But what if directors see that the discerners are not tranquil and so cannot use their natural powers freely and tranquilly? The Official Directory answers: "If anyone does not have this tranquility, it is better that he continue with his meditations until the storm passes and peace returns, because as long as water is troubled, nothing can be seen clearly in it."[12]

Are the discerners in fact in this tranquil time? Most often, directors and discerners will sense together whether or not this is so. Should, however, discerners believe they are in this tranquil time and their directors judge otherwise, the directors will share this perception with the discerners and delay third-mode discernment. Juanes proposes the following: "A norm that appears prudent and opportune might be this: as long as it is not sure beyond all reasonable doubt that the person is in a true Ignatian tranquil time, the person should not be advised to discern by the third mode."[13]

In this case, as the Official Directory indicates, directors should invite discerners to continue with their daily meditation, review of prayer, examen prayer, and spiritual direction, "until the storm passes and peace returns." When directors judge that discerners have attained the tranquil time, they will invite the discerners to begin third-mode discernment.

Third-Mode Discernment: First Way

The third mode, Ignatius writes, "is one of tranquility, when one *considers* first for what *purpose man is born*, that is, to praise God our Lord and save his soul, and, *desiring* this, chooses as a *means to this end* some life or state within the bounds of the Church, so that he may be helped in the service of his Lord and the salvation of his soul" (*SpirEx*, 177). From the outset, Ignatius recalls the foundation: those who undertake third-mode discernment begin by *considering* the foundation of all true discernment—that we are created to praise, reverence, and serve God and so attain eternal life (*SpirEx*, 23)—and by *desiring* to discern according to this truth. With the foundation clarified and desired, the choice assumes its truth as a *means* to *this end*. As we will see, when Ignatius describes the concrete practice of third-mode discernment, he will explicitly urge discerners to have only this end in view as they discern.

Ignatius supplies two ways of doing third-mode discernment. In this chapter, we will explore the first. We will introduce it through a contemporary's description of Ignatius's own practice of this first way. In his biography of Ignatius, Jesuit Pedro de Ribadeneyra recounts:

> When he wrote the Constitutions and when he decided something of great weight and importance, as we said, he always first consulted with the Lord about it in prayer, and the way he did this was the following. First he emptied himself of any passion or attachment that often confuse and obscure judgment, such that it cannot discover so easily the radiance and light of the truth, and he placed himself, without any fixed inclination or predetermined direction, like matter ready to take any shape, in the hands of God our Lord. After this, with great energy he asked of God grace to know and to embrace the better choice. Then he considered with great attentiveness and weighed the reasons that presented themselves for one option and for the other, and the strength of each, and he compared them among themselves. Finally, he turned again to our Lord with what he had thought and what he had found, and reverently placed it all before his divine gaze, beseeching

him that he would give him light to choose what would be most pleasing to him.[14]

Ignatius considered with great attentiveness and weighed "the reasons that presented themselves for one option and for the other." He did this when his heart was tranquil and in a spirit of much prayer. This account exemplifies the practice that Ignatius codified in the *Spiritual Exercises* as the *first way* of doing third-mode discernment.

In the *Spiritual Exercises*, Ignatius articulates this first way through a series of points. We will examine each by exploring his words and in the light of his own practice as described here. Directors must assimilate well these points and explain them clearly to those who undertake this first way of doing third-mode discernment. Such explanation is the directors' first task when inviting discerners to third-mode discernment.

First Point: The Question

The first point, Ignatius says, "is to place before myself the thing about which I wish to make a choice." The first need is *to see clearly the options in the choice.* For Ignatius in his discernment regarding poverty, the options are radical poverty or a poverty mitigated for the sake of churches entrusted to the Jesuits. As is evident, the two options are clearly defined. Such clarity renders third-mode discernment possible; without it, the discernment lacks a necessary presupposition and is unlikely to lead to a sound conclusion. Richard discerns between married life with a career in business and Jesuit religious life. Again the options are clear, and the discernment can proceed on sure ground.

But if a man, for example, attempts to discern between a career in medicine or law and has only an imperfect knowledge of both—he does not have the relevant data—his discernment will flounder. If a woman seeks to discern between options for a graduate degree but does not know which options are in fact open to her, her discernment likewise will flounder. Fessard writes: "Ignatius begins by asking that the person place before himself the object of the choice. Many deliberations . . . go quickly astray because they lose from sight their object! 'What is the issue here?' is the first, fundamental question."[15] Casanovas adds more simply, "The first point determines and fixes the matter of the choice."[16]

Directors, therefore, when beginning third-mode discernment with discerners, must verify that these perceive clearly the options in the choice: Are they properly prepared for this discernment? Have they researched the options? Do they have *all the relevant data*?[17] Are the options clearly defined? If so, they may proceed with third-mode discernment. If not, more preparation is required before effective third-mode discernment is possible.

Second Point: The Disposition

When the options are clear, Ignatius turns immediately to the *disposition* necessary for discernment. Once more he reminds discerners that "it is necessary to have as my objective the end for which I am created, that is, to praise God our Lord and save my soul" (*SpirEx*, 179). At the outset of third-mode discernment, therefore, directors should invite discerners to consider explicitly *this end* toward which their choice is to be a *means*.

Ignatius describes in detail the disposition that results and that permits effective third-mode discernment: "I must be indifferent [available to God, desiring only God's will], without any disordered attachment, so that I am not more inclined or disposed to accept the thing before me than to refuse it, nor to refuse it rather than accept it, but that I find myself like a balance at equilibrium, ready to follow whatever I perceive to be more for the glory and praise of God our Lord and the salvation of my soul" (*SpirEx*, 179). *Like a balance at equilibrium*: the metaphor aptly describes the necessary disposition. Discerners must be available to God, free of disordered attachments—as, for example, a person who desires one option because people will think well of him, because he does not want to change his present circumstances, because the other option would mean less income, and the like—and open to either option should God reveal it to be his will. Ribadeneyra tells us that when Ignatius approached discernment, "he placed himself, without any fixed inclination or predetermined direction, like matter ready to take any shape, in the hands of God our Lord." *Like matter ready to take any shape*: this metaphor too describes well the disposition.

As time allows and as directors judge helpful, they may invite discerners to repeat one or more texts prayed earlier when seeking this disposition. Those supplied in Chapter 2 under the heading "Availability to God in the Discernment" and those given in Chapter 4 under the heading "Meditations for Seeking the Helpful Disposition" may be of assistance. Directors may also suggest a prayerful rereading of Ignatius's text (*SpirEx*, 23).[18] They will judge what may be helpful according to individual discerner's needs.

Directors must verify that discerners in fact possess this disposition. As we have said, this cannot be taken for granted. The absence of this disposition renders true discernment impossible; its presence permits fruitful discernment.

Third Point: The Petition

Discerners now turn to prayer of petition. The next step, Ignatius says, is *"to ask God our Lord* that he be pleased to *move my will* and *place in my soul* what I ought to do in the matter before me that would be more for his praise and glory" (*SpirEx*, 180). Ribadeneyra tells us that when Ignatius had placed himself before God like matter ready to take any shape, "with great energy he asked of God grace to *know* and to *embrace* the better choice." Ignatius asks discerners to pray for this same double grace—for a mind that sees clearly and a will that chooses according to God's will. The one discerning, Ignatius writes, asks for the grace of "using my *intellect* well and faithfully to weigh the matter, and *choosing* in accord with what is pleasing to his most holy will" (*SpirEx*, 180).

Directors will invite discerners to spend time in such prayer. Before looking at the advantages and disadvantages of the options, discerners might dedicate several days to this prayer, according to individual need. They might use the text of Ignatius's third point (*SpirEx*, 180) as the basis of a petition expressed in their own words. They might also pray with apposite scriptural texts, as for example:

- the delight in God's will expressed in Psalm 40:6–8
- Abraham's availability to God (Genesis 12:1–9)

- Solomon's prayer for wisdom (Wisdom 9:1–18)
- Jesus' constant availability to his Father's will (John 4:34, 6:38, 8:29; Matthew 26:36–46; Romans 5:19; Hebrews 10:5–10)
- Mary's yes to God's plan (Luke 1:26–38)
- Paul's total openness to Christ (Philippians 3:1–11)

These and similar passages may aid the discerners' prayer of petition.

Directors aid discerners at this point by inviting them to engage in this prayer and by suggesting ways of doing it. Directors will also judge when the prayer is sufficiently complete—when, to use Ribadeneyra's description of Ignatius, discerners have asked God with great energy for the grace to know his will and embrace it.

This step powerfully indicates that third-mode discernment is *an exercise of prayer* and not simply one of human prudence in which persons seek wise decisions in choices they face. As Juanes writes, "The entire process of deliberation—before, during, and after—should be 'wrapped' in prayer to the Lord."[19] Directors will assist discerners, as Juanes says, to envelop the entire process of third-mode discernment in prayer.

Fourth Point: The Reasons

After these preparatory steps, Ribadeneyra tells us, Ignatius "considered with great attentiveness and weighed *the reasons* that presented themselves for *one option* and for *the other*, and the strength of each, and he compared them among themselves." At this point in third-mode discernment, Ignatius writes, the discerner considers "by way of reasoning" the *advantages and disadvantages* "solely for the praise of God our Lord and the salvation of my soul" (*SpirEx*, 181) of *both options*. When directors sense that discerners grasp both options clearly (first point), are now "like a balance at equilibrium" (second point), and have prayed sincerely for God's help (third point), the directors will invite them to examine the *advantages and disadvantages* for God's greater glory of the *one option and the other* (fourth point). Generally they will do this through the method of the four columns, listing in writing the advantages and disadvantages for God's greater glory of the one option (two columns) and of the other (two columns).[20]

Throughout third-mode discernment, discerners should continue their daily time of prayer. Their directors will invite them to dedicate a part of this prayer to considering the advantages and disadvantages for God's greater glory of both options. Thus, for example, discerners may dedicate thirty minutes of their hour of prayer to this consideration for several days or their full hour of prayer on alternating days. They may make a day of retreat during third-mode discernment and dedicate two or three times of prayer on that day to this consideration. Through these practices or other variations of them as coordinated with their directors, they will dedicate time to this consideration.[21] Directors may also invite discerners, as their occupations permit, to consider these advantages and disadvantages outside the formal times of prayer.[22]

Discerners must note not simply the number of advantages and disadvantages for either option but also the weight of each: Ignatius "*weighed* the reasons that presented themselves for one option and for the other, and *the strength of each*, and he *compared them* among themselves." The Official Directory comments: "The advantages and disadvantages of the course under deliberation should be set forth separately, each point then being carefully weighed and examined to see toward which side the balance inclines."[23] One or two advantages, for example, of one option may have greater weight than a number of disadvantages; conversely, one or two disadvantages may weigh significantly in the choice.

Sampaio adds a further consideration: "This pondering of concrete motives must be guided by *two criteria* to be applied together: the weight of greater service [of God] and the concrete reality of the person. What is objectively for greater service may not be so subjectively."[24] Directors must help discerners to consider both criteria as they ponder the advantages and disadvantages of the options: Will this option, for example, of great value for God's glory in itself, be so for *this discerner* in his or her concrete spiritual, psychological, physical, familial, educational, ethnic, financial, and social circumstances?

Ignatius writes that the advantages and disadvantages considered must be "solely for the praise of God our Lord and the salvation of my soul" (*SpirEx*, 181). These are spiritual, faith-based reasons that aim, as Ignatius's signature phrase indicates, at God's greater glory.[25]

González Dávila highlights this quality: "Note that all the reasons or advantages that are envisaged and move to a given choice ought to derive from the already mentioned principle of the love of God."[26] The Official Directory repeats this emphasis: "The one thing to be observed and practiced here is . . . that the reasons adduced in the deliberation must all proceed from the principle of the divine service. No considerations of human respect or worldly advantage should be admitted here."[27]

As directors accompany discerners in third-mode discernment, the directors must note whether the reasons listed are truly faith-based reasons for God's greater glory—reasons that indicate that this choice will serve to make God more known and loved. As always, God's greater glory, his praise and service, and by this means the discerners' eternal salvation are the *end* toward which the option is chosen as the better *means*. Any reasons deriving from desire for material comfort, worldly esteem, or similar motives must be identified as such and excluded.

The directories repeatedly urge that the advantages and disadvantages of the options be listed *in writing*—the four columns already mentioned.[28] The Official Directory affirms this counsel and explains why: "The person should also be told to write down in separate columns the reasons that occur to him on either side. When all the reasons on either side are lined up together, they make the truth more evident and have stronger motivating force. The person should lay these reasons before the director so that he can guide him better."[29]

Directors, therefore, should invite discerners to write the advantages and disadvantages as these occur to them in prayer and reflection. Directors will also invite discerners to share these written reasons in their meetings of direction. The written columns will be an invaluable tool both for the discerner—the columns "make the truth more evident and have stronger motivating force"—and the director, since when the discerner shares the columns, the director "can guide him better."

Fifth Point: The Choice

"After I have thought and reasoned in this way about every aspect of the thing before me," Ignatius writes, "I will look to see toward which alternative reason inclines more." "In this way," he continues, "according to the greater movement of reason, and not through any sensual inclination, *I should come to a decision* about the matter under deliberation" (*SpirEx*, 182).

After the diligent search for advantages and disadvantages of the preceding point, discerners are ready to examine the options to see which God wills—which presents more advantages for God's greater glory, that is, which will serve more to make God known and loved. They do this according to the *greater movement of reason*: if God is giving them third-mode discernment, then as they prayerfully review the columns of advantages and disadvantages, their human reason, enlightened by faith and the Holy Spirit, will perceive which option better serves God's glory.

Ignatius specifies that this choice is to be made according to the greater *movement of reason*, and not through any *sensual inclination*.[30] If, for example, a man is discerning whether God wants him to remain in software design or pursue studies in medicine, he might find the following "advantages" inclining him to choose medicine: "If I become a doctor, people will look up to me more, and I will finally gain the respect I've long wanted in life. If I become a doctor, I'll have a comfortable lifestyle with a nice house, car, and vacations." In Ignatius's terms, a choice for medicine because of these "advantages" would arise not from the movement of reason but from a *sensual inclination*. Directors, therefore, must note whether discerners engaged in third-mode discernment choose according to the movement of reason enlightened by faith or out of such sensual inclinations. If directors perceive that discerners have chosen according to such sensual inclinations, they must help the discerners to grasp this and invite them to examine their choice anew.

When discerners have made their choice, they bring it to their directors. The directors, Sampaio writes, "will *judge the rectitude* of the decision made by the person."[31] Calveras elaborates: "The director, on his part, will not approve the choice until he sees clearly that the person has followed the process well in everything, and after he has shared the reasons that move him and the decision he has reached."[32] In this judgment, directors will ask themselves questions such as these: Have the discerners verified well the advantages and disadvantages of both options? Have they perceived clearly the weight of these

advantages and disadvantages? Have they reasoned well or has emo-
tion clouded their reasoning? If directors judge that the choice has
been made well, the discernment may proceed to its final step.

Sixth Point: The Confirmation

When Ignatius made his choice, Ribadeneyra writes, "Finally, he turned
again to our Lord with what he had thought and what he had found,
and reverently *placed it all before his divine gaze,* beseeching him that
he would give him light to choose what would be most pleasing to him."
When Ignatius has identified the choice that will serve God's greater
glory, he brings this choice before God and seeks God's *confirmation*
of it. In the *Spiritual Exercises,* Ignatius writes: "Having made this
choice or deliberation, the person who has made it should, with much
diligence, turn to prayer before God our Lord and *offer him this choice,*
so that his Divine Majesty may be pleased to receive and *confirm* it, if it
is for his greater service and praise" (*SpirEx,* 183). When, therefore, the
discerners have reached a choice that their directors judge well made,
their directors should invite them to pray for such confirmation.

Directors, consequently, will encourage discerners to present their
choice to God in prayer, asking that God confirm it. In this prayer,
discerners ask God to confirm that they have reasoned well and have
found the choice that will serve for his greater glory. They may do this
during their daily time of prayer, simply presenting to God the choice
made, asking for his confirmation of it, and noting what then arises
in their minds and hearts. When in prayer, they may also review the
reasons that led to this choice to see if God will give even greater light
or reveal further reasons supporting the choice.[33] Directors may suggest scriptural texts that help discerners seek this confirmation, or
propose other ways of seeking it in prayer.[34] Directors will judge how
best to propose this prayer for confirmation to individual discerners.

As discerners share their experience of this prayer, directors will
watch for *signs* of God's confirmation. These may be of several kinds,
and discerners may experience one or more of these:

- Experiences of warm and joyful *spiritual consolation* as discern-
  ers present their choice to God.
- Perception of *new reasons* supporting this choice.
- *Greater strength in reasons already seen.*

- A *stronger drawing of the will* in glad desire for this choice.
- An *increased readiness to act* upon the choice.
- A *peaceful assurance that the process has been done well*, that nothing more remains to be done, and that God's will has indeed been found.[35]

Directors will watch for these and similar signs of God's confirmation as discerners share their experience of prayer.

How long should discerners persist in this prayer for confirmation? Ignatius asks that discerners make this prayer "with much diligence" (*SpirEx*, 183), indicating that some measure of time and energy should be dedicated to it.[36] How long precisely will depend on several factors. The more important the choice—a vocational discernment, for example, or a significant change in career—the more time should be dedicated to seeking God's confirmation. Less time may be required for choices of lesser import. The time available for the discernment may also influence how much time is spent seeking confirmation, as, for example, when a person is discerning a job offer with a deadline for acceptance or refusal. The strength or lack of strength of the signs given will likewise guide a director's sense of when this search is complete: should discerners receive abundant and strong signs of confirmation, less time will be necessary; if fewer and less clear signs are given, more time will be required. Ultimately, as Toner writes, "it is a matter of good judgment" on the part of directors.[37]

Various outcomes may flow from this prayer for confirmation, and the directories provide counsel to directors regarding each. Polanco offers the most complete treatment of this matter, and we will follow his exposition.[38] He first reminds directors that "any movements or enlightenments from above which he [the discerner] experiences in prayer should be examined by the Rules for Discernment of Spirits."[39] Polanco then explores four possible scenarios:

First scenario: discerners pray for confirmation of the choice they have made, and signs of the good spirit are detected: discerners experience "inward movements and lights from above," indicating that God approves the choice and promises strength to carry it out. Such movements and lights are "an excellent sign" and should be taken as God's seal on the choice made. In the discerners' prayer, God has confirmed the choice.

Second scenario: discerners pray for confirmation of the choice they have made and experience "movements, feelings, or intellectual lights" that weaken the choice. When, however, these movements and lights are examined by the rules for the discernment of spirits, they are seen to be of the enemy, or at least not clearly of God and possibly of the enemy.[40] In this case, the choice should not be changed "since this kind of temptation might be the work of the demon."

Third scenario: discerners pray for confirmation of the choice they have made, and there is clear evidence of interior movements and intellectual lights from the good spirit that opposes the choice made. This is a sign that the reasoning process of third-mode discernment was not done well, and the choice must be made again. In the discerners' prayer, God has not confirmed the choice.

Fourth scenario: discerners pray for confirmation of the choice they have made but experience no noteworthy interior movements or intellectual lights. Their wills, however, remain firm in the choice made.[41] In this case, they should not change the choice they have made but should conclude that God wanted his will to be known through rational reflection—the preceding points of third-mode discernment.

If, Polanco adds, the *second way* of doing third-mode discernment (*SpirEx*, 184–88) is employed and results in the same choice as this first way, "he [the discerner] should be all the more convinced that he has found God's will." We will explore this second way of doing third-mode discernment in the next chapter.

Polanco's list of scenarios provides valuable practical counsel for directors. It indicates once again that directors must know well the rules for the discernment of spirits and know how to apply them to discerners' experiences.

Third-Mode Discernment: An Example

Patrick shares his story:

> I had always worked in business, at one point managing twenty branches of my company. About ten years ago, I began doing prison ministry as a volunteer. I enjoyed this service, and as the years passed, increased the time I dedicated to it. This ministry awakened my interest in theology, and over several

years I completed a master's degree in theology in the diocesan program for laity.

A year after I began prison ministry, my company downsized, and I lost my job. When that happened, I began my own consulting business.

Things went along this way for several years until the sister who ran prison ministry for the diocese was transferred by her community, and her position became open. The diocese offered me the position, and I said no. I liked prison ministry but wanted to remain a part-time volunteer.

Soon, however, I began to feel unsettled, unsure of whether my answer had been right. No one had been appointed to the position, and I knew that if I changed my answer, the diocese would be glad to accept me. I had prayed for many years, but I didn't know how to discern. So I spoke with a spiritual director and asked his help. He agreed and asked me to spend an hour a day in prayer. My parish had a Blessed Sacrament chapel, and I decided I would pray there. The director gave me scriptural texts for the prayer and asked that I jot down what happened each day as I prayed. I began doing this and meeting with the director to discuss the prayer.

How will his director accompany Patrick in this discernment? For our purposes here, we will assume that as two or three weeks pass, the director sees no clear signs of first- or second-mode discernment. Time is not unlimited, since, if Patrick delays too long, the position may be closed. The director, therefore, decides to invite Patrick to third-mode discernment. How will the director proceed? His guide will be Ignatius's six points (*SpirEx*, 178–83).

Patrick's prayer in the preceding weeks has already helped prepare third-mode discernment. His director has explained the foundation (Chapter 2 above), invited Patrick to surrender any disordered attachments (Chapter 3) and described both the necessary and the helpful dispositions (Chapter 4). The director has given Patrick scriptural texts to seek these graces, and Patrick has prayed them with good will and fruit. If time permitted, the director might extend this preparatory phase, but Patrick's decision must be made in a few weeks. Trusting, therefore, that God asks only our best in the concrete circumstances, the director now invites Patrick to undertake third-mode discernment.

The director will verify that Patrick grasps the question clearly (first point): Does he perceive the two options clearly, and does he have the relevant data? The answer is yes. The first option is to continue his consulting business and remain a volunteer in prison ministry; the second is to serve as director of prison ministry for the diocese. Patrick understands this latter option well both from his experience in management and his years of prison ministry. Patrick, then, possesses the relevant data for both options: their respective demands in time and energy, level of stress, financial implications, and impact on his family. He is ready to proceed in third-mode discernment.

The director will attend to Patrick's disposition in this choice (second point): Is Patrick's end (goal) in this choice to praise God and attain eternal life, and does he see this choice as a *means* to *this end*? Is he like a balance at equilibrium, ready to follow whatever he perceives to be more for the glory and praise of God our Lord and his eternal salvation? As best he can in the time available, the director will help Patrick to grow in this disposition.

The director will invite Patrick to ask God for help in the discernment he is about to make (third point). The director may suggest that Patrick dedicate his hour of prayer to this petition for the next two or three days, supplying ways of making this prayer.

The director will explain the four columns and suggest that for several days Patrick dedicate his hour to prayerful reflection on the advantages and disadvantages for God's greater glory of both options (fourth point). He will counsel Patrick to list these in writing. When Patrick considers that he has done his best with this, he will share the four columns with his director. The director will help verify the faith-based quality of the advantages and disadvantages listed—that they have God's greater glory in view—and that Patrick has considered well the necessary issues.

When Patrick has made his choice (fifth point), he will bring this to his meeting with his director. Patrick, for example, may have found the advantages for God's greater glory of taking the position compelling: he knows prison ministry well; he possesses the necessary administrative skills; his theological studies will enrich his service;

and he will be giving more of himself to the Lord. He may find the disadvantages of taking the position—reduced time for himself, surrender of a more comfortable life, and similar considerations—of less weight by comparison. If so, the "greater movement of reason" indicates that God wills Patrick to accept the position offered.

The director will attend carefully to Patrick's explanation of his choice. If the director judges that Patrick has reasoned well and made his choice "according to the greater movement of reason, and not according to any movement of sensuality," he will invite Patrick to seek God's confirmation of this choice. If not, the director will ask Patrick to continue to explore and evaluate the advantages and disadvantages of both options until his choice appears well made.

When the director judges that Patrick's choice is well made, he will invite Patrick to dedicate several days, according to need, to seeking God's confirmation (sixth point). The director will supply Patrick with means for this prayer and will guide him through it. According to its outcome (Polanco's four scenarios), the director will either prolong or conclude the search for confirmation and so the discernment itself. Thus, when Patrick presents the new position to God in prayer, he may find himself consoled, see new reasons why this position will better serve God's glory, find himself desiring it more, and feel a peaceful assurance that the discernment has been made well and is clear. If such experiences emerge, the director will recognize the signs of God's confirmation and that the discernment is complete. Patrick may now tell the diocese that he accepts the position, confident that he has found God's will.[42]

Third-Mode Discernment, First Way: A Director's Checklist

When directors accompany discerners in such third-mode discernment, the following questions will assist them:

- Before undertaking third-mode discernment, have the directors verified that *God has not given the discerners first- or second-mode discernment?*[43] In some circumstances, time may not permit the complete process of second-mode discernment. If times does permit and in any case, before proceeding to third-mode discernment, directors must examine whether or not God has given first- or second-mode discernment.

- Are the discerners in a *tranquil time* and able to use their natural powers freely and tranquilly? Or are they agitated by different spirits?
- Do the discerners *see the question clearly*? Do they know both options well? Do they possess the relevant data?
- Do the discerners see this choice as a *means* to the *end* (goal) of praising God and attaining eternal salvation? Are they seeking God's greater glory in this choice—what will make God more known and loved in human hearts?
- Do the discerners have the necessary *disposition*? Are they like a balance at equilibrium, ready to follow either option should God reveal it to be his will?
- Before reviewing the advantages and disadvantages of both options, have the discerners *prayed* from their hearts, asking God to guide their minds and wills in this discernment?
- Have the discerners prayerfully considered and listed the *advantages and disadvantages* of both options (the four columns)? Are these faith-based advantages and disadvantages, seen as such in the light of *God's greater glory*? Have the discerners considered the weight of each? Have they written the list of advantages and disadvantages? Have they shared these with their directors?
- Have the discerners made a *choice* "according to the greater movement of reason, and not through any sensual inclination"? Have their directors judged the rectitude of this decision and guided the discerners accordingly, either approving the choice or asking them to reexamine it as necessary?
- Have the discerners sought God's *confirmation* of this choice in prayer? Have they received signs of that confirmation? Have their directors guided them in this according to what emerges from this prayer?
- Do the directors judge that the discerners would benefit from the *second way* of doing third-mode discernment (*SpirEx*, 184–88) as a complement to this first way?

This last question introduces our next chapter. There we will examine Ignatius's final approach to discerning God's will.[44]

Chapter Nine

A Preponderance of Reasons

The Third Mode (II)

The love that moves me and causes me to choose this thing
must descend from above, from the love of God.
                                        —St. Ignatius of Loyola

After proposing the first way of doing third-mode discernment, Ignatius continues: "Lastly, one may use the way that is given after this
of four points, as the last that may be used."[1] This final approach is
the *second way* of doing third-mode discernment, outlined according
to the four rules Ignatius supplies in the *Spiritual Exercises* (*SpirEx*,
184–88). In this approach, Ignatius asks once again that discerners
verify their disposition (first rule) and then provides three tests to help
them examine their choice objectively: what counsel they would give
to *a person they do not know* and who is faced with their same choice
(second rule); what choice they will wish to have made *when life is
ending* (third rule); finally, what choice they will wish to have made *in
the light of eternity* (fourth rule).

When should directors propose to discerners this second way
of doing third-mode discernment? As we have just seen, Ignatius
describes this second way as "the *last* that may be used." The second
way, therefore, presumes that the first has already been employed.
Discerners have examined the advantages and disadvantages for
God's glory of both options but have not found the full clarity they
need. In this case, directors are to propose the second way. If discerners have reached clarity through the first way, directors may judge

nonetheless that this second way will strengthen that clarity and so may propose it to discerners.[2]

Ignatius's order—*first* way, *second* way—is important. The second way comes after the first and presupposes its careful review of advantages and disadvantages. Without this solid grasp of the issues involved, the three tests of the second way will lack their necessary basis and so cannot bear fruit. Consequently, directors will propose the second way only after the first way and as they judge it helpful for individual discerners.

Presenting the Second Way

The second way, Ignatius tells us, "contains four rules and a note" (*SpirEx*, 184). We will look at each of these and at how directors should present them.

First Rule: The Disposition

At the outset of the second way, Ignatius reaffirms the disposition necessary for discernment: "The first is, that *the love that moves me* and *causes me to choose* this thing must descend from above, *from the love of God*; so that the one who chooses should first of all feel in himself that the love, greater or lesser, that he has for the thing he chooses, *is solely for the sake of his Creator and Lord*" (*SpirEx*, 184). When, therefore, directors invite discerners to undertake the second way, the directors will first ask them to verify that their motive for choosing a particular option "descends from above, from the love of God," that is, that this motive is rooted only in the love of God. The one who chooses, Ignatius emphasizes, should *first* feel in himself that the love he has for a given option—the man, for example, who is discerning between software design and studies in medicine and feels drawn to medicine—is solely for the sake of his Creator and Lord.

This first rule, Toner writes, is "plainly yet another insistence on purity of heart and indifference to all motives apart from the love of God."[3] Toner aptly comments: "Ignatius urges over and over again the necessity of these dispositions for beginning and continuing and concluding any choice by any mode."[4] Ignatius's constant return to the disposition alerts directors to its importance throughout the entire discernment.

Directors, therefore, adhering to Ignatius's first rule, will once more present the disposition to discerners who undertake the second way. Discerners may wish to pray with Ignatius's text (*SpirEx*, 184), to engage in prayer of petition for this disposition, or to repeat scriptural texts already found fruitful in seeking it (Chapter 2, "Availability to God in the Discernment" and Chapter 4, "Meditations for Seeking the Helpful Disposition"). Discerners must ask: Is the love I have for this option from the love of God, and is it solely for the sake of my Creator and Lord? Directors will help discerners ask this question, pray for this grace, and will verify with them that this grace is sufficiently present to permit second-way discernment.

Polanco comments on Ignatius's insistence that the discerner "should first of all feel in himself that the love . . . he has for the thing he chooses, *is solely for the sake of his Creator and Lord*," and specifies: "If love for God, while being the chief motive, is nevertheless not the sole one but is accompanied by other motives in favor of the same choice which do not conflict with the love or God and are good in themselves—v.g., one's own spiritual consolation, considerations of health, or the like—this is no reason for condemning the choice. However, the other motives besides God himself should not be the chief ones, and ought themselves to be subordinated to love of God."[5]

Second Rule: A Person I Have Never Seen

A first test follows. In this test, Ignatius says, I "look at *a person whom I have never seen or known*, and, *desiring all perfection for him*, consider what I would tell him to do and to choose for the greater glory of God our Lord and the greater perfection of his soul; and, doing myself the same, *follow the rule that I propose to the other*" (*SpirEx*, 185). Directors will explain that discerners are to consider another person faced with their same choice, as, for example, the man choosing between software design and medicine. Moreover, this other person is one whom the discerners *do not know* such that family relations or friendship will not confuse their consideration. The test is simple: If discerners desire all perfection for this person, that is, all holiness and all love and service of God, what choice would they advise him or her to make? What choice do discerners see as better serving God's glory

and the holiness of this person? Then, Ignatius writes, let the discerners make that same choice.

This test is "a device for gaining objectivity and honesty with oneself"[6] in the choice faced. It helps remove any "rationalization spring-
ing from my desires and fears"[7] since I consider not my own situation
but that of another whose full service of God and holiness I desire.

Third Rule: When Life Is Ending

Ignatius then supplies a second test. In this test, I "consider, as if
I were at *the point of death,* what procedure and norm of action *I
would then wish to have followed* in making the present choice; and,
guiding myself by this, *make my decision entirely in conformity with
it*" (*SpirEx*, 186).

This test, like the preceding, situates discerners at a point—when
life is ending—in which all lesser motivations will lose their force
and all that will matter will be to have loved God and served his
greater glory. At that time, and viewed with that clarity, what choice
will discerners wish to have made in the present discernment? Discerners, Ignatius writes, should make that same choice now.[8] This
test, too, helps discerners view their discernment objectively and so
with clarity.

Fourth Rule: In the Light of Eternity

Ignatius proposes one final test. Discerners see themselves on the
day of judgment and consider how, at that time, they will wish to
have chosen in the present discernment. Again, Ignatius writes, they
should make that same choice now (*SpirEx*, 187).

Directors may explain that the judgment is not between eternal
loss and eternal life. Discerners are not choosing between good and
evil, but between two goods, one of which will better promote God's
glory. The judgment will concern whether, in this choice, I have loved
fully the One who loves me infinitely, or whether I have loved with
reservation. The desire I will then feel to have loved fully, Ignatius
says, will assist me to choose now with unreserved love.[9] Once again,
a simple but powerful exercise helps discerners gain objectivity and so
greater freedom in choosing as God desires.[10]

A Note: The Confirmation

When the choice has been made, discerners are to seek God's confirmation of it (*SpirEx*, 188). All that we have said about such confirmation in the first way (sixth point) applies here as well: "Having made this choice ... the person who has made it should, with much diligence, turn to prayer before God our Lord and offer him this choice, so that his Divine Majesty may be pleased to receive and confirm it, if it is to his greater service and praise" (*SpirEx*, 183).[11] Directors need only recall for discerners the explanation of confirmation they gave earlier when the discerners employed the first way of third-mode discernment. The search for God's confirmation is equally important in the second way and here, as in the first way, must be made "with great diligence."

Polanco suggests that discerners dedicate an hour to praying with each of these four rules.[12] Directors will adapt this or similar counsels to the needs of individual discerners.

Can one rule—one of these tests—suffice of itself or must all four always be employed? Casanovas offers a balanced reply: "Each of these rules is of itself sufficient to provide the answer in the choice proposed, but by applying all four, the person remains more satisfied with the result, which in any case will always be the same."[13] Directors again will adapt this position to the needs of individual discerners.

Discerners may at times experience the second way as "a more brilliant and rapid light" than the first way.[14] The first way requires patient gathering of advantages and disadvantages and careful weighing of them until a judgment emerges: this is the option that will better serve God's glory. Yet discerners praying, for example, with the first test in the second way—asking themselves what choice they would counsel another facing their same choice—at times may instantly or almost instantly recognize what they would tell that person: of the two, this is the option that will better serve God's glory.[15] The wisdom of Ignatius's order, that the second way follows the first, is apparent. The quick perception the second way may permit presupposes the careful review of advantages and disadvantages in the first way. The second way can be effective only after the first way and should not be attempted until after the first way has been used.

The Second Way: Mark's Story

Mark shares his experience:

> I married in my late twenties, and my wife Denise and I had three children. My career has been in human relations, and I have worked for several companies in this field. In my early forties, I began to feel the call to be a deacon. My wife agreed, and when I was forty-seven, I was ordained a permanent deacon.
>
> My bishop assigned me to a large parish, where I served as deacon, preaching, doing baptisms, weddings, and burial services. In addition, because of my business background, I was asked to help with the parish school and the renovation of the church building. I loved all this service and, as my children grew older, was able to give more time to it. The various projects went well, and the parish grew. But after thirteen years of this service, together with my human relations job and the needs of the family, I found myself deeply tired. I remember one evening when I first began to wonder whether I could continue as deacon in this parish or whether I might need a change.
>
> I spoke about this with my spiritual director, and he encouraged me to let the bishop know my situation. A few weeks later, I did speak with the bishop, and it was a good conversation. He knew about my situation. He told me that he was happy with my work in the parish and that if I wanted to continue, that would be fine. But he also said that he saw my tiredness and that he wanted me to discern what I thought I should do. He would honor whatever decision I would make. I spoke with Denise, who was aware of my deep tiredness. She agreed with the bishop and encouraged me to discern the best choice.
>
> The bishop's response was heartening, and I was willing to discern. Still, to discern about a position I'd had for so long was not easy for me. When I met with my spiritual director, he told me not to try to discern right away—that the issue was to become free enough to choose well. So I continued to pray

daily, and we continued to meet. About five weeks later, when we met, he thought I was free enough to discern whether I should stay at the parish or ask for another assignment. He suggested that I continue to pray, and that we would see what emerged from my prayer. For the next few weeks, I did this.

No clarity, at least not enough to make a choice, seemed to come from this prayer and so the director suggested that I try St. Ignatius's third mode of discernment. A week later, I did try it. I sat in the church with a notebook and wrote down the advantages I could see in staying on in this parish and the disadvantages. I did the same with the possibility of taking another assignment from the bishop. When I considered everything—the fact that I had been in this parish for thirteen years and had given pretty much all that I could; the effort it was costing me now just to do the daily work of a deacon there; the real danger that, if I tried to continue, I was likely to get dangerously exhausted and have to stop anyway; the fact that things were in good shape and that there were others who could now step in; my sense that I could do more good by a change that would help me start again with new energy rather than dragging in my work the way I was doing—it seemed to me that the greater good was to have someone else take over and that I get a fresh start in another assignment. As far as I could see, following St. Ignatius, this was saying that God's will was that I should ask the bishop for another assignment. But I still wasn't sure, and I wasn't ready to act.

I shared all of this with my spiritual director, and he suggested that I now try the second way St. Ignatius gives. About three days later, I did that in the same chapel. When I took the second point—where you think of another person facing the same decision and what you would say to that person—it really hit me. I knew immediately that I would never ask another person to continue in the same ministry with such deep exhaustion. I don't think I ever went beyond this first consideration in the second way. This was so clear that I felt I had my answer.

When I shared this with my spiritual director a few days

later, he agreed that this seemed very clear. He suggested that I now take this choice to the Lord in prayer and ask the Lord for confirmation. When I did that, within a few days I started to feel real happiness, a deep peace about the discernment, a certainty that I was doing God's will. I spoke with Denise, and she agreed. The director now thought the discernment process was concluded, that there was nothing more that needed to be done, and that it was time to speak with the bishop.

A few days later, I did. The bishop agreed with the discernment and thought that the reasons sounded right. It was the final piece in the discernment and confirmed my sense that I had found God's will. This was the point I had always wanted to reach in the whole process.[16]

When Mark approaches his spiritual director, the director does not invite him to begin discerning immediately but rather suggests a time of preparation, that is, that the first issue is "to become free enough to choose well." Mark knows that since he has invested so much of himself for so many years in the parish, the discernment will not be easy. The director wisely provides time for Mark to grow in the disposition that permits effective discernment.

After five weeks of prayer, the director judges that Mark now possesses this disposition and so invites him to direct his daily prayer toward the discernment itself. Several weeks pass, and "no clarity, at least not enough to make a choice, seemed to come from this prayer." The director recognizes that God has not given first- or second-mode clarity and, since time is not endless in this discernment, judges that Mark should now undertake third-mode discernment.

The director invites Mark to employ the first way, the review of advantages and disadvantages for God's greater glory. Mark does this well and finds that the preponderance of reasons suggests that a new assignment will better serve God's glory. Yet, Mark adds, "I still wasn't sure, and I wasn't ready to act."

This is precisely the situation for which Ignatius offers the second way: when the first way has been attempted, and though some light has emerged, some unclarity also persists.[17] The director recognizes this, and proposes the second way to Mark.

When Mark prays with the second way, the first of the three tests, "where you think of another person facing the same decision and what you would say to that person," speaks deeply to him. In his business career, Mark's work in human relations has led him to counsel many in similar decisions regarding employment. When he applies the first test, Mark knows "immediately that I would never ask another person to continue in the same ministry with such deep exhaustion." Mark never even considers the remaining two tests. The first "was so clear that I felt I had my answer."

When Mark shares the results of the first test with his director, the director has a choice. The director may judge that the first test is so clear that Mark need not employ the second and third. This is the approach Mark's director takes. The director, however, if he considers it helpful for Mark, may counsel Mark to employ the second and third tests as well. As Casanovas writes, "By applying all four [rules] the person remains more satisfied with the result, which in any case will always be the same." Directors will decide this question as seems best in the concrete circumstances of the individual.

Mark's director now invites him to pray for God's confirmation of his choice. Mark does, and "within a few days I started to feel real happiness, a deep peace about the discernment, a certainty that I was doing God's will." When Mark shares this experience with his director, the director recognizes the signs of God's confirmation. Mark's interior confirmation is strengthened by his wife's agreement with his choice. When he speaks with his bishop, Mark receives the confirmation of Church authority, an external confirmation necessary for his assignment as a deacon.

At this point, Mark's discernment is complete. His experience illustrates the fruitfulness of Ignatius's second way and why Ignatius offers it to discerners.

Foods to a Prince

Having described the second way as "the last that may be used,"[18] Ignatius adds a further consideration: "One could also present *one option* to God our Lord *on one day* and *the other* on *the next*, as for example the counsels [religious life] on one day and on the next the precepts [lay vocation], and observe *toward which of these* God our

Lord *gives a greater indication of his divine will,* like one who presents different foods to a prince and observes which of these pleases him."[19]

In this text, Ignatius supplies directors with another tool that may assist them in accompanying discerners. The directors, for example, of the woman discerning between teaching in the prestigious high school or the inner-city high school for disadvantaged children, of Patrick discerning between his own business or serving as director of prison ministry, or Mark as he discerns between his present assignment or serving in another parish, may find this tool helpful for these discerners.

Thus, the teacher's director might invite her to present the one option and the other to God on successive days for a week or longer, as time allows and as seems helpful, and to watch "toward which of these God our Lord gives a *greater* indication of his divine will." On one day, for example, in her hour of prayer she might offer to God the position in the prestigious high school with the good she can accomplish there and the benefits for her family and career. As she reviews her prayer, she will attend to any indications—experiences of spiritual consolation, compelling reasons, or other signs—God may give that this option is his will. Her director may also invite her to present this option to God at other times of prayer in the day—when she is at Mass or prays Morning Prayer from the Liturgy of the Hours or says the Rosary—or in free moments during the day, again watching for any indications that this option is God's will. On the following day she can do the same for the position in the inner-city high school and the good she can accomplish there for the disadvantaged students.[20] As she alternates these options day after day, she will look to see toward which God gives a *greater* indication of his will. Patrick's and Mark's directors, if they judge this helpful, may also invite them to do the same.

Ignatius advisedly writes, "One *could* also present. . . ."[21] This approach is an option to be used or not used as directors judge helpful.

The Official Directory describes the dispositions with which discerners should employ this approach: "There is another procedure for doing this given by our Father Ignatius under his image of a person who offers a certain kind of food to his prince to see how he likes it. In a similar way, the soul, with deep humility and fervent love and a desire to please God, may offer him at different moments first one thing and then the other, watching to see which of them is more acceptable and pleasing to him, saying always, 'Lord, what would you have me do?' [Acts 9:6]. The person should say and feel this not just with his lips or only a slight affection of his mind, but with his whole heart, indeed with many hearts if he had them."[22] If directors invite discerners to adopt this procedure, they may propose these dispositions to the discerners.

Third-Mode Discernment, Second Way: A Director's Checklist

When directors accompany discerners in the second way of third-mode discernment, the following questions will assist them:

- Are the discerners in a *tranquil time* and able to use their natural powers freely and tranquilly? Or are they agitated by different spirits?
- Have the discerners employed the first way of doing third-mode discernment (the four columns)? Have they explored well the advantages and disadvantages of both options for God's greater glory?
- Do the directors judge that the first way has not brought full clarity and that more must be done to complete the discernment? If so, the directors will propose the second way.[23]
- Have the discerners verified that the love they have for a given option descends from the love of God and is solely for the sake of their Creator and Lord (first rule)?
- Have they unhurriedly and prayerfully employed the three tests: the choice they would advise another to make, the choice they will wish to have made when life is ending, and the choice they will wish to have made in the light of eternity? Have one or more of these tests brought clarity?
- Have they sought God's confirmation of their choice? Has God given that confirmation? Through what signs?

- Do their directors judge that they have employed well the four rules and final note of the second way (*SpirEx*, 184–88)? Do the directors judge that the choice made was clear and that God's confirmation has been given?
- Does the choice resulting from this second way harmonize with that of the first way? Such harmony is "a good sign of a good choice."[24]
- Do the directors judge that presenting the options to God on successive days may help the discerners? If so, for which option has God given greater indication that it is his will?

Chapter Ten

After the Choice

May He deign in his infinite and supreme goodness to give us his abundant grace to know his most holy will and perfectly to fulfill it.

—St. Ignatius of Loyola

Ignatius's emphasis on the disposition required before undertaking the three modes indicates that "the discerner must have already chosen in principle and have a firm will to carry out whatever the discernment process will lead him to judge is God's will."[1] Nonetheless, discerners will benefit if their will to act is "stabilized and confirmed"[2] after they have made their choice. Courage may be required to do what they now know God wills.

Directors will assist discerners, therefore, if they provide discerners with means for this strengthening of the will. If time and geographical proximity allow, directors and discerners may continue to meet during this final phase. If not, directors may supply means for such strengthening before the discerners depart or continue to meet through the means of social communication during this final phase.

Ignatius finds in the passion and resurrection of Jesus the ideal scriptural focus for this strengthening.[3] As they judge opportune, directors may propose to discerners the contemplation of Jesus who fulfills the Father's will in a suffering that leads to new life. As discerners contemplate Jesus' suffering and the new life arising from it, they will be strengthened to do God's will in the choice just made.

Following Ignatius's lead, I provide a sample of scriptural texts that directors may offer to discerners. Directors may use these or other texts as they judge helpful for individual discerners.

The Suffering of Jesus

Luke 22: 7–27	Jesus gives himself completely, body and blood.
John 13:1–17	He loved them to the end.
Matthew 26:36–46	Not my will but yours be done.
Luke 23:1–25	Jesus is unjustly condemned.
John 19:17–37	Jesus gives his life on the cross.
Psalm 22	I am poured out like water.
Isaiah 52:13–53:12	By his wounds we are healed.
Philippians 2:6–11	Obedient unto death.

The Rising of Jesus

Matthew 28:1–10	He has risen as he said.
John 20:11–18	Woman, why are you weeping?
Luke 24:13–35	Did not our hearts burn within us?
John 20: 19–23	Peace be with you.
John 21:1–19	Do you love me?
Matthew 28:16–20	I am with you always.
Psalm 118	I shall not die, but live.
2 Corinthians 1:3–11	The God of all consolation.
Ephesians 3:20–21	God who is able to do far more than we can ask.
John 14:12–31	The Father will give you another Counselor.

At this point, we have completed the trajectory of discernment: laying the foundation, removing the obstacles, forming the disposition, applying the three modes of discernment, and, finally, strengthening the will to act. Directors now possess the essential instruction Ignatius wishes to provide them.

In our exposition of these various steps, at times we have touched on broader issues, not confined to specific stages in the process. Our reflections would be incomplete without an explicit consideration of these issues. In the following sections, we will present and briefly discuss each.

Qualities of the Director

The directories offer multiple counsels to directors regarding how they are to interact with discerners. Several qualities emerge.

"With God's Own Goodness"

The Official Directory describes a discerner "who is not prompt in responding to God's call," and who "seems not to respond to God's will with much readiness, or to overcome himself as he ought."[4] How should the director respond to such a discerner? The Directory affirms that "he [the discerner] still should be patiently borne with in hopes that gradually and step by step he will overcome the obstacles in his way. In this we ought to imitate the way of acting of God's own goodness, of which we are collaborators, for he disposes all things sweetly, and perseveringly waits out the soul's delays in coming to him."[5]

González Dávila discusses the hesitations discerners may experience when God's will becomes apparent. At this point, he says, discerners may struggle and delay. He writes: "Note that at these critical moments we should not overwhelm the person who is making the choice, and should not be constantly pushing him. He needs to catch his breath sometimes and not constantly be under such pressure that 'such a one may be swallowed up with sorrow' [2 Cor 2:6]. For if his heart once fails, it is hard to restore his courage."[6]

The Official Directory adds that the director "should be kindly rather than austere, especially toward persons suffering from temptations, desolations, aridity, or weariness. These he ought to console, inspire, and encourage with suitable counsel and advice, as well as by his own and others' prayers."[7] The Directory's encouragement to pray personally for the discerner and to ask others to pray is worthy of note.

The various directories' calls to patience and goodness apply to the time of discernment Ignatius's general counsel that when a discerner is "desolate and tempted," the director "should not be hard and sharp with him, but gentle and kind, giving him courage and strength for the future, and revealing to him the devices of the enemy of human nature, and preparing and disposing him for the consolation that will come" (*SpirEx*, 7). As the Official Directory states, in the delicate task of accompanying discernment, directors "ought to imitate the way of acting of God's own goodness, of which we are collaborators."[8]

Avoid Precipitation

Ignatius enjoins directors that if the discerner "goes on with consolation and much fervor, he [the director] should alert him not to make any inconsiderate and precipitous promise or vow; and the more he knows him to be inconstant of character, the more he should alert and admonish him" (*SpirEx*, 14). In such cases, Ignatius continues, one "should note carefully the individual's condition and personal qualities, and how much help or difficulty he will find in fulfilling the thing he wishes to promise" (*SpirEx*, 14).[9] When discerners are tempted and desolate, their directors are to give them courage and strength; when discerners experience abundant and ongoing consolation, their directors are to watch that no ill-considered steps be taken.

The Official Directory repeats this caution: "In moments of ardor or consolation vows are often made that are regretted later. This precaution needs to be taken especially with persons of ardent, hasty, or unstable character."[10] Paul Hoffaeus adds: "When the person is in deep consolation and fervor, he should avoid making any sudden, unconsidered promise or vow. Careful attention must be given to all the positive and negative factors that might affect the execution of what he is about to promise."[11] The directors' role includes such vigilance when discerners experience times of rich consolation.

"Let the Creator Work Immediately with the Creature"

The directors' role changes when discerners move from preparation for discernment to discernment itself. During the preparation, Iparraguirre notes, directors actively assist discerners to attain the disposition required for discernment—the necessary disposition (like a balance at equilibrium) and, if possible, the helpful disposition (a positive inclination toward the poverty and humility of Christ).[12] Directors supply apposite scriptural texts for prayer and accompany discerners as they seek this disposition. They help incline discerners' hearts toward this disposition.

Once, however, discerners have attained this disposition and enter discernment itself, the directors' role changes. Directors are to explain the modes of discernment and show discerners how to proceed. Having done this, Iparraguirre continues, directors are to withdraw and allow God to work directly in the discerners' hearts.[13] *Before* the discernment, directors *help incline discerners' hearts* toward the needed *disposition*; *during* the discernment—when utilizing the three modes—they carefully *avoid inclining discerners' hearts* toward either *option*. At this point, as Ignatius writes, they "allow the Creator to work directly with the creature, and the creature with his Creator and Lord" (*SpirEx*, 15).[14]

Directors guide discerners in employing the three modes, help them apply the rules for discernment, encourage them as needed, and alert them to possible pitfalls. They accompany, but they never come between God and the discerner. They incline to neither option in the choice discerners face but are like a balance at equilibrium: they allow God to work directly with the discerners.

Questions and Answers

In this final section, we will address a number of remaining questions. Our focus throughout will be practical: How are directors to understand these issues, and what are they to do when these arise?

Should Second-Mode and Third-Mode Discernment Be Used Together?

When a second-mode discernment is not clear, directors invite discerners to undertake third-mode discernment. What if, however, the second-mode discernment does appear to be clear? Is the discernment finished? Or should directors invite discerners even in this case to employ third-mode discernment as a further confirmation of the second-mode discernment? Is this superfluous—the second-mode discernment appears to be clear of itself—or is it wise practice to apply the light of reason to confirm a discernment made through spiritual movements (consolation and desolation)? Said differently, does God, who asks that we do our best to discern, desire that we use this further means even when the second-mode discernment seems clear?

The Ignatian tradition has long debated this question.[15] Those who consider this practice unnecessary point to Ignatius's language in the *Spiritual Exercises* and *Autograph Directory*, the two places where Ignatius addresses the three modes.[16] In neither document does

Ignatius indicate that third-mode discernment is to be applied when second-mode discernment is clear. On the contrary, his clear supposition is that each mode is autonomous: if the discernment is made in the first mode, the other modes are not necessary; if in the second, the third is not necessary; and if not in the second, then the third is to be used.

Those who consider this practice wise, however, point to Ignatius's *Spiritual Diary* and his discernment regarding poverty described there. In this discernment, Ignatius employed both second- and third-mode discernment, seeking God's will through spiritual movements (second mode) and through reason enlightened by faith (third mode). Ignatius's practice, these commentators affirm, indicates the wisdom of using third-mode discernment to confirm a second-mode discernment even when this seems clear—as was Ignatius's second-mode discernment regarding poverty. Ignatius wished the peace of knowing he had done all he could to discern God's will. He would, these commentators teach, desire that other discerners experience this same peace.[17]

Both opinions may be found in the early directories.[18] Sampaio offers the following general summary: "These [directories] consider that, though it is not always necessary to use the third mode, it may be helpful to use it to gain greater surety regarding the discernment made previously by the second mode."[19]

In practice, then, what are directors to do? I believe that this must depend on the judgment of directors in individual cases. Several factors may influence this judgment.

The more important the discernment, the more likely directors will be to propose third-mode discernment even when the second-mode discernment seems clear.[20] Thus both director and discerner may have the peace of knowing that everything possible to discern God's will in an important matter has been done.

Polanco describes an instance in which a second-mode discernment appears to contradict what reason sees regarding the choice. He advises directors that "in cases where a person inclined to what is more perfect makes a discernment that is apparently against reason, the discernment should be tested by the first and second way of the third mode (and not merely by the rules for the discernment of spirits), for the greater satisfaction of director and discerner."[21] Thus, if a second-mode discernment appears to be made well but also appears to contradict what reason sees in the choice, directors should propose third-mode discernment to the discerner for greater security in the discernment.

Polanco proposes a further case: What if directors suggest the third-mode to discerners who have made a second-mode discernment, though with "some doubt whether the movement was from God,"[22] and the results of the third mode contradict those of the second? Polanco replies, "In the case where one choice is made during the second mode, and then, there being some doubt whether the movement was from God, the two ways of the third mode are proposed and result in the contrary choice, the two choices should be carefully tested by means of the rules for discerning spirits, by right reason, and by sound doctrine. The motives impelling either way should be weighed."[23]

Different outcomes may result from this weighing. First, "If it is quite clear that reason is in favor of the choice made in the third mode, it is safer to go with the latter [the choice made in the third mode], because of the director's uncertainty whether the movements in the second mode were from God or not." If the third-mode discernment is very clear, it is to be followed rather than a second-mode discernment regarding which some doubt remained.

Second, "On the other hand, if the reasons in favor of the discernment in the third mode are weak, and the movements of the second mode emerge more clearly as deriving from the good spirit and are not in conflict with right reason, then preference should be given to the discernment made in the second mode." In this case, the conclusion of the third-mode discernment is weak, and as the discerner proceeds in this testing, the spiritual movements of the second mode emerge more clearly as of God. When this occurs, the second-mode discernment is to be followed.

What if all of this has been done, and clarity has not resulted? Cordeses replies: "If the issue remains doubtful, the discernment should be made over again."[24]

What If More Than One Choice Must Be Made?

At times, discerners may face complex discernments that include several significant choices. They may feel unsure of how to proceed and look to their directors for help. How may directors proceed? When Ignatius describes vocational discernment, he provides a model for how directors may choose to approach such situations.[25]

The one discerning his vocation, Ignatius writes, should first discern whether God is calling him to the evangelical counsels (vows of poverty, chastity, and obedience) or to the lay state.[26] If he perceives that God is calling him to the evangelical counsels, he may proceed to a second discernment: Does God will that he live the evangelical counsels in religious life or outside of religious life? If he understands that God is calling him to religious life, a third discernment follows: Which religious institute does God will that he enter? Once this is clear, he faces a fourth and final discernment: When does God will that he enter this institute, and how should he proceed toward entering?[27] The directories repeat this counsel of discernment by progressive stages in such cases.[28] Ignatius emphasizes, González Dávila writes, "that the discernment has to follow this sequence step by step and not be made all at once, or we will be overwhelmed."[29]

Ignatius's procedure provides directors with an approach they may adopt if they judge it helpful. Adequate research—into job offers or career choices, for example—often will narrow the options. Should the choice remain complex, however, and if time allows, directors may invite discerners to discern the choices in sequence. Directors will judge in individual cases whether this procedure or some adaptation of it may assist discerners.

What Kind of Certitude Does Discernment Give?

Ruiz Jurado answers succinctly: discernment permits us to recognize God's will "with the certitude necessary for human moral activity."[30] Toner writes of "Ignatius's belief in God's guiding our sound discernment so that we do find his will and can have a justifiable faith-conviction that we have found it,"[31] and again of "Ignatius's ground for giving certain assent to the finalized conclusion of a sound discernment process."[32] Toner, following Ignatius, carefully qualifies this conviction: such certain assent presumes two conditions essential for any sound discernment—that discerners possess the necessary disposition (openness to the Holy Spirit) and have done their reasonable best to find God's will (dedicated use of the means available to them).[33]

Toner describes the "ground" for Ignatius's confidence that sound discernment truly does find God's will. The evidence that results from the three modes is essential to discernment; on it is based our *conclusion* about God's will in the discernment. Our justifiable *certitude* of having found God's will, however, is based not on this evidence but on our trust that God, out of the love he bears for us, will lead those who with well-disposed hearts do their best to seek his will.[34]

González Dávila elaborates: "This is the satisfaction possessed by the soul enabling it to trust much in God, who will not let it be deceived; for since it is seeking him with all its heart, it will find him. And we can believe nothing else of this divine goodness than that he will welcome whoever so truly seeks him, since he goes out to meet even those who do not seek him."[35] In similar language, the Official Directory affirms that when a person seeks only God's glory, "it gives him great confidence that God will not let him be deceived. For whenever anyone seeks God truthfully and wholeheartedly, God will never turn away from him, seeing that his goodness and love for his creatures are so great that he often comes forth to meet even those who do not seek him."[36]

Discerners must approach discernment with the necessary disposition (like a balance at equilibrium) and, if possible, the helpful disposition (a positive inclination of heart toward the poverty and humility of Christ) as well. They must also do their best to discern, using the spiritual means available to them.[37] When they have attained this disposition and have done their best in the process, Ignatius believes that God's help will not be lacking, and they can be justifiably certain that the conclusion reached is God's will. His confidence that this conclusion is God's will is based on his faith-conviction that God, who loves his sons and daughters so deeply, will not disappoint their sincere efforts to find his will through sound discernment.

The director's responsibility is evident. Directors must assist discerners to attain the requisite disposition and guide them through a sound process of discernment—that is, they must ensure that the essential conditions for sound discernment are present. Having done this, directors and discerners may be justifiably certain that God's will has been found.[38]

We must note that certitude about the choice does not predict what will actually happen when the person puts the choice into action. As Toner writes, "What God wills actually to happen as consequences of the discerner's decision and free choice is beyond the limits of discernment."[39]

Through a well-made discernment, for example, a man may reach certitude that God wills him to pursue a career in medicine. God clearly wills, then, that he do all he can to attain this goal. Whether or not he will actually achieve a career in medicine is beyond the limits of his discernment of God's will. He may very likely become a doctor and serve God in this way throughout his life. But if, for example, struggles of health surface subsequently and he is unable to complete his studies in medicine, this does not negate the soundness of the discernment made earlier. It simply means that God willed him to choose a career in medicine and do his best to pursue it.[40] In pursuing this career, even though later obstacles render it impossible, he has done what God willed him to do. In so doing, he may be confident that God will bless him through these efforts—through these studies, for example, he may meet his future wife or be prepared for a paramedical career that opens new ways to serve God at home or in the third world.

The certitude reached through well-made discernment is the certitude that God wants the discerner to make this choice and to pursue it with energy. What will then happen is beyond the limits of the discernment and lies in the heart of the God, who knows how to give good things to his children (Matthew 7:11).

What If the Discerner Still Does Not Have an Answer? A Director's Checklist

Finally, what if all that we have described has been done, and the discerner still has not found clarity? Such is unlikely to be common, but it may occur. When facing this situation, directors may find the following checklist helpful:

- Is the one discerning *psychologically* and *spiritually* ready to discern? Have any significant psychological wounds impeded the process? Should this person pursue psychological growth before attempting this specific discernment? Does this person need deeper spiritual formation—a truer image of God, fuller understanding and capacity for prayer, and so forth—before attempting this specific discernment?

- Do I as director understand sufficiently the forms of *Ignatian prayer*—meditation, contemplation, repetition, review of prayer, and the examen? Do I know the two sets of *rules for the discernment of spirits* sufficiently well to guide the discerner in their application?

- Do I as director understand sufficiently well the *three modes of discerning God's will*? Do I know how to guide the discerner in their use?

- Have I asked the discerner to pray with the *foundation*? Have I ensured that, in the measure possible, the discerner has assimilated this foundation and built the discernment upon it?

- Have I encouraged the discerner to *remove the obstacles* to discernment—in Ignatius's vocabulary, any "disordered affections"? Have I invited the discerner to seek in prayer a growing freedom from sinfulness and to experience God's love and mercy in that place of vulnerability?

- Before applying the three modes, have I assisted the discerner to attain the necessary disposition (like a balance at equilibrium) and if possible the helpful disposition (a positive inclination of heart toward the poverty and humility of Christ) as well? Has the discerner *attained this disposition* in the measure possible and sufficiently to enter discernment?

- Have I watched to see whether God has given a *first-mode* clarity beyond doubting?

- Have I been attentive to the discerner's experiences of spiritual consolation and desolation? Have I proposed to the discerner one or more ways of employing *second-mode* discernment? Have I watched to see whether God has given the discerner sufficient clarity and understanding through spiritual consolation and desolation? Have I helped the discerner apply the rules for the discernment of spirits to these? Have I perceived when the first set of rules applies and when the second?

- If the second-mode has not brought clarity, have I proposed *third-mode* discernment to the discerner? Have I explained this well and accompanied the process? If the first way (four columns) has not brought clarity, have I proposed the second way (three tests)?

Should the answers to these questions be affirmative, and still clarity has not been reached, the call is to persevere. After describing the second way of doing third-mode discernment, Sampaio writes: "If not even this has brought enough light to conclude the discernment, it is necessary to be persevering and patient, believing that God, sooner or later, will show us his will. For our part, we are asked only to dispose ourselves as best we can to receive the manner and time in which God will choose to reveal himself to us."[41] A warm confidence in God's faithful love for both discerner and director is the final word in discernment.

Text of the Principle and Foundation

Original Text[1]

Man is created to praise, reverence, and serve God our Lord, and by this means to save his soul.

The other things on the face of the earth are created for man to help him in attaining the end for which he is created.

Hence, man is to make use of them in as far as they help him in the attainment of his end, and he must rid himself of them in as far as they prove a hindrance to him.

Therefore, we must make ourselves indifferent to all created things, as far as we are allowed free choice and are not under any prohibition. Consequently, as far as we are concerned, we should not prefer health to sickness, riches to poverty, honor to dishonor, a long life to a short life. The same holds for all other things.

Our one desire and choice should be what is more conducive to the end for which we are created.

A Contemporary Reading[2]

God created us out of love so that we might praise and reverence his infinite love and goodness, and by dedicating our lives to his service, might enter an eternity of joyful communion with him.

God created all the other things on the earth for us, to help us attain this purpose for which he created us.

As a result, we should appreciate and use these gifts of God—places, occupations, relationships, material possessions, and all the other blessings of God's creation—insofar as they help toward the purpose for which we are created, and we should let them go insofar as they hinder our attainment of this purpose.

Consequently, in choices in which we are free to choose among various options, we must hold ourselves as in a balance with regard to these gifts of God's creation. This means that for our part we do not set our desires on health rather than sickness, wealth rather than poverty, being held in honor rather than in little esteem, a long life rather than a short life, and likewise in all the rest.

Our only desire and choice is for what better leads us to the purpose for which God created us: to praise and serve him in this life, and so enter the joy of eternal life.

Appendix Two

Ignatius's Text on Making a Choice[3]

Three Times in Any of Which a Sound and Good Choice May Be Made

The first time is when God our Lord so moves and attracts the will that, without doubting or being able to doubt, the devout soul follows what is shown to it, as St. Paul and St. Matthew did in following Christ our Lord. (175)

The second time is when sufficient clarity and understanding is received through experience of consolations and desolations, and through experience of discernment of different spirits. (176)

The third time is one of tranquility, when one considers first for what purpose man is born, that is, to praise God our Lord and save his soul, and, desiring this, chooses as a means to this end some life or state within the bounds of the Church, so that he may be helped in the service of his Lord and the salvation of his soul. I said a tranquil time, that is, when the soul is not agitated by different spirits and uses its natural powers freely and tranquilly. (177)

If the choice is not made in the first or second time, two ways of making it in this third time are given below. (178)

The First Way to Make a Sound and Good Choice Contains Six Points

First Point. The first point is to place before myself the thing about which I wish to make a choice, such as an office or a benefice[4] to be accepted or refused, or any other thing that may be the object of a choice that can be changed.[5]

Second Point. The second. It is necessary to have as my objective the end for which I am created, that is, to praise God our Lord and save my soul. In addition, I must be indifferent, without any disordered attachment, so that I am not more inclined or disposed to accept the thing before me than to refuse it, nor to refuse it rather than accept it, but that I find myself like a balance at equilibrium, ready to follow whatever I perceive to be more for the glory and praise of God our Lord and the salvation of my soul. (179)

Third Point. The third. To ask God our Lord that he be pleased to move my will and place in my soul what I ought to do in the matter before me, that would be more for his praise and glory, using my intellect well and faithfully to weigh the matter, and choosing in accord with what is pleasing to his most holy will. (180)

Fourth Point. The fourth. To consider by way of reasoning how many advantages or benefits accrue to me if I have the office or benefice proposed, solely for the praise of God our Lord and the salvation of my soul; and, on the contrary, to consider in the same way the disadvantages and dangers there would be in having it. Then to do the same in the second part, that is, to look at the advantages and benefits in not having it, and, in the same way, at the disadvantages and dangers in not having it. (181)

Fifth Point. The fifth. After I have thought and reasoned in this way about every aspect of the matter before me, I will look to see toward which alternative reason inclines more; and, in this way, according to the greater movement of reason, and not through any sensual inclination, I should come to a decision in the matter under deliberation. (182)

Sixth Point. The sixth. Having made this choice or decision, the person who has made it should, with much diligence, turn to prayer before God our Lord and offer him this choice, so that his Divine Majesty may be pleased to receive and confirm it, if it is to his greater service and praise. (183)

The Second Way to Make a Sound and Good Choice Contains Four Rules and a Note

First Rule. The first is, that the love that moves me and causes me to choose this thing must descend from above, from the love of God;

so that the one who chooses should first feel in himself that the love, greater or lesser, that he has for the thing he chooses is solely for the sake of his Creator and Lord. (184)

Second Rule. The second, to look at a man whom I have never seen or known, and, desiring all perfection for him, consider what I would tell him to do and to choose for the greater glory of God our Lord and the greater perfection of his soul; and, doing myself the same, follow the rule that I propose to the other. (185)

Third Rule. The third, to consider, as if I were at the point of death, what procedure and norm of action I would then wish to have followed in making the present choice; and, guiding myself by this, make my decision entirely in conformity with it. (186)

Fourth Rule. The fourth, looking and considering how I will find myself on the day of judgment, to think of what decision I would then wish to have made about the present matter; and to adopt now the rule that I would then wish to have followed, so that then I may find myself in full satisfaction and joy. (187)

Note. Taking the above-mentioned rules for my salvation and eternal peace, I will make my choice and my offering to God our Lord, in accordance with the sixth point of the first way of making a choice. (188)

Appendix Three

The Rules for the Discernment of Spirits

First Set of Rules[6]

Rules for becoming aware and understanding to some extent the different movements that are caused in the soul, the good, to receive them, and the bad to reject them. And these rules are more proper for the first week. (313)

First Rule. The first rule: In persons who are going from mortal sin to mortal sin, the enemy is ordinarily accustomed to propose apparent pleasures to them, leading them to imagine sensual delights and pleasures in order to hold them more and make them grow in their vices and sins. In these persons the good spirit uses a contrary method, stinging and biting their consciences through their rational power of moral judgment. (314)

Second Rule. The second: In persons who are going on intensely purifying their sins and rising from good to better in the service of God our Lord, the method is contrary to that in the first rule. For then it is proper to the evil spirit to bite, sadden, and place obstacles, disquieting with false reasons, so that the person may not go forward. And it is proper to the good spirit to give courage and strength, consolations, tears, inspirations and quiet, easing and taking away all obstacles, so that the person may go forward in doing good. (315)

Third Rule. The third is of spiritual consolation. I call it consolation when some interior movement is caused in the soul through which the soul comes to be inflamed with love of its Creator and Lord, and, consequently, when it can love no created thing on the face of the earth in itself, but only in the Creator of them all. Likewise when it sheds tears that move to love of its Lord, whether out of sorrow for one's sins or for the passion of Christ our Lord, or because of other things directly ordered to his service and praise. Finally, I call consolation every increase of hope, faith, and charity, and all interior joy that calls and attracts to heavenly things and to the salvation of one's soul, quieting it and giving it peace in its Creator and Lord. (316)

Fourth Rule. The fourth is of spiritual desolation. I call desolation all the contrary of the third rule, such as darkness of soul, disturbance in it, movement to low and earthly things, disquiet from various agitations and temptations, moving to lack of confidence, without hope, without love, finding oneself totally slothful, tepid, sad, and as if separated from one's Creator and Lord. For just as consolation is contrary to desolation, in the same way the thoughts that come from consolation are contrary to the thoughts that come from desolation. (317)

Fifth Rule. The fifth: In time of desolation never make a change, but be firm and constant in the proposals and determination in which one was the day preceding such desolation, or in the determination in which one was in the preceding consolation. Because, as in consolation the good spirit guides and counsels us more, so in desolation the bad spirit, with whose counsels we cannot find the way to a right decision. (318)

Sixth Rule. The sixth: Although in desolation we should not change our first proposals, it is very advantageous to change ourselves intensely against the desolation itself, as by insisting more upon prayer, meditation, upon much examination, and upon extending ourselves in some suitable way of doing penance. (319)

Seventh Rule. The seventh: Let one who is in desolation consider how the Lord has left him in trial in his natural powers, so that he may resist the various agitations and temptations of the enemy; since he can resist with the divine help, which always remains with him, though he does not clearly feel it; for the Lord has taken away from him his great fervor, abundant love, and intense grace, leaving him, however, sufficient grace for eternal salvation. (320)

Eighth Rule. The eighth: Let one who is in desolation work to be in patience, which is contrary to the vexations which come to him, and let him think that he will soon be consoled, diligently using the means against such desolation, as is said in the sixth rule. (321)

Ninth Rule. The ninth: There are three principal causes for which we find ourselves desolate. The first is because we are tepid, slothful, or negligent in our spiritual exercises, and so through our faults spiritual consolation withdraws from us. The second, to try us and see how much we are and how much we extend ourselves in his service and praise without so much payment of consolations and increased graces. The third, to give us true recognition and understanding so that we may interiorly feel that it is not ours to attain or maintain increased devotion, intense love, tears, or any other spiritual consolation, but that all is the gift and grace of God our Lord; and so that we may not build a nest in something belonging to another, raising our mind in some pride or vainglory, attributing to ourselves the devotion or the other parts of the spiritual consolation. (322)

Tenth Rule. The tenth: Let the one who is in consolation think how he will conduct himself in the desolation that will come after, taking new strength for that time. (323)

Eleventh Rule. The eleventh: Let one who is consoled seek to humble himself and lower himself as much as he can, thinking of how little he is capable in the time of desolation without such grace or consolation. On the contrary, let one who is in desolation think that he can do much with God's sufficient grace to resist all his enemies, taking strength in his Creator and Lord. (324)

Twelfth Rule. The twelfth: The enemy acts like a woman in being weak when faced with strength and strong when faced with weakness. For, as it is proper to a woman, when she is fighting with some man, to lose heart and to flee when the man confronts her firmly, and, on the contrary, if the man begins to flee, losing heart, the anger, vengeance, and ferocity of the woman grow greatly and know no bounds, in the same way, it is proper to the enemy to weaken and lose heart, fleeing and ceasing his temptations when the person who is exercising himself in spiritual things confronts the temptations of the enemy firmly, doing what is diametrically opposed to them; and, on the contrary, if the person who is exercising himself begins to be afraid and lose heart in suffering the temptations, there is no beast so fierce on the face of the earth as the enemy of human nature in following out his damnable intention with such growing malice. (325)

Thirteenth Rule. The thirteenth: Likewise he conducts himself as a false lover in wishing to remain secret and not be revealed. For a dissolute man who, speaking with evil intention, makes dishonorable advances to a daughter of a good father or a wife of a good husband, wishes his words and persuasions to be secret, and the contrary displeases him very much, when the daughter reveals to her father or the wife to her husband his false words and depraved intention, because he easily perceives that he will not be able to succeed with the undertaking begun. In the same way, when the enemy of human nature brings his wiles and persuasions to the just soul, he wishes and desires that they be received and kept in secret; but when one reveals them to one's good confessor or to another spiritual person, who knows his deceits and malicious designs, it weighs on him very much, because he perceives that he will not be able to succeed with the malicious undertaking he has begun, since his manifest deceits have been revealed. (326)

Fourteenth Rule. The fourteenth: Likewise he conducts himself as a leader, intent upon conquering and robbing what he desires. For, just as a captain and leader of an army in the field, pitching his camp and exploring the fortifications and defenses of a stronghold, attacks it at the weakest point, in the same way the enemy of human nature, roving about, looks in turn at all our theological, cardinal, and moral virtues; and where he finds us weakest and most in need for our eternal salvation, there he attacks us and attempts to take us. (327)

Second Set of Rules[7]

Rules for the same effect with greater discernment of spirits, and they help more for the second week. (328)

First Rule. The first: It is proper to God and to his angels, in their movements, to give true joy and spiritual gladness, taking away all sadness and disturbance that the enemy induces; to whom it is proper to militate against that joy and spiritual consolation, bringing apparent reasons, subtleties, and persistent fallacies. (329)

Second Rule. The second: It is of God our Lord alone to give consolation to the soul without preceding cause; because it is proper to the Creator to enter, go out, to move it interiorly, drawing it totally in love of his divine majesty. I say without cause, without any previous sentiment or knowledge of some object, through which such a consolation comes, by means of its acts of understanding and will. (330)

Third Rule. The third: With cause both the good angel and the bad can console the soul, for contrary ends: the good angel for the profit of the soul, that it may grow and rise from good to better; and the bad angel for the contrary, and later on to draw it to his damnable intention and malice. (331)

Fourth Rule. The fourth: It is proper to the bad angel, who takes on the appearance of an angel of light, to enter with the devout soul and to go out with himself; that is, to bring good and holy thoughts, conformed to such a just soul, and afterward, little by little, he endeavors to go out, bringing the soul to his hidden deceits and perverse intentions. (332)

Fifth Rule. The fifth: We should give much attention to the course of the thoughts; and if the beginning, middle, and end is all good, inclined to all good, it is a sign of the good angel; but if in the course of the thoughts that he brings, it ends in something bad, or distractive, or less good than the soul had proposed to do before, or if it weakens it, or disquiets, or troubles the soul, taking away the peace, tranquility, and quiet, which it had before, it is a clear sign that it proceeds from the bad spirit, the enemy of our profit and eternal salvation. (333)

Sixth Rule. The sixth: When the enemy of human nature has been perceived and known by his serpent's tail and the bad end to which he induces, it profits the person who was tempted by him to look immediately at the course of the good thoughts that he brought, and the beginning of them, and how little by little he procured to make him descend from the sweetness and spiritual gladness in which he was, till he brought him to his depraved intention; so that with such an experience known and noted he may guard himself in the future from his customary deceits. (334)

Seventh Rule. The seventh: In those who proceed from good to better, the good angel touches such a soul sweetly, lightly, and gently, as a drop of water that enters a sponge; and the bad touches it sharply and with noise and disquiet, as when the drop of water falls on a stone; and in those who proceed from bad to worse the above-said spirits touch in a contrary way; the cause of which is that the disposition of the soul is contrary or similar to the said angels; for when it is contrary, they enter with clamor and sensible disturbances, perceptibly; and when it is similar, they enter with silence, as in their own house through an open door. (335)

Eighth Rule. The eighth: When the consolation is without cause, although there is no deception in it, since it is of God our Lord alone, as has been said, nevertheless the spiritual person to whom God gives such a consolation should, with much vigilance and attention, look at and distinguish the time itself of such an actual consolation from the time following, in which the soul remains warm and favored with the favor and remnants of the past consolation; for frequently, in this second time, through his own reasoning by associating and drawing consequences from ideas and judgments, or through the good spirit, or through the bad, he forms different proposals and opinions that are not given immediately by God our Lord; and therefore they must be very well examined before entire credit is given them or they are put into effect. (336)

Appendix Four

Resources for Directors and Discerners

Space in this book has not permitted a thorough treatment of Ignatian prayer and the rules for the discernment of spirits. As mentioned, to have provided such a treatment would have expanded this book to several volumes. For a full discussion of Ignatian meditation and contemplation, the examen prayer, and the two sets of rules for the discernment of spirits, I refer directors and discerners to my other Ignatian titles. I believe that these books can assist directors in preparing to accompany discernment of God's will. I believe also that they provide a ready means for discerners to grow in their ability to employ these Ignatian "tools." I provide here a brief summary of each title and a reference to the corresponding digital resources.

Books

The Discernment of Spirits: An Ignatian Guide for Everyday Living (New York: Crossroad, 2005)
This book explores the first set of rules for the discernment of spirits. It helps readers to understand clearly what Ignatius means by "spiritual consolation" and "spiritual desolation," and how to respond to both. This set of fourteen rules presumes that the enemy is attempting to deceive through the discouragement of spiritual desolation, and equips discerners to recognize and reject this tactic of the enemy. Knowledge of these rules is an invaluable aid for discerning God's will. This book also supplies directors with a practical means for presenting them to discerners.

Spiritual Consolation: An Ignatian Guide for the Greater Discernment of Spirits (New York: Crossroad, 2007)
This second book provides the same service for the eight rules of the second set. Here the enemy is attempting to mislead discerners

through deceptive spiritual consolation. These eight rules supply an effective roadmap through this complex issue of discernment.

The Examen Prayer: Ignatian Wisdom for Our Lives Today (New York: Crossroad, 2006)
This book offers directors and discerners an accessible treatment of the daily examen prayer and equips discerners to pray it during their time of discernment and after. The examen helps discerners grasp God's action not only in formal prayer but throughout the day as well. It alerts them to any discouraging and misleading traps of the enemy in the day. Such awareness greatly assists discernment.

Meditation and Contemplation: An Ignatian Guide to Praying with Scripture (New York: Crossroad, 2008)
This book introduces discerners to Ignatian prayer with Scripture, equipping them for reflective prayer (meditation) and imaginative prayer (contemplation) with Scripture. It provides a flexible under-standing of these approaches—how to begin, how to pray during the body of the prayer, how to conclude, and how to review the prayer—to help them pray during their discernment and beyond.

An Ignatian Introduction to Prayer: Scriptural Reflections According to the Spiritual Exercises (New York: Crossroad, 2008)
This little book presents forty scriptural texts for prayer chosen according to the Spiritual Exercises. They are lightly developed to help discerners grow in Ignatian prayer with Scripture. If time permits and the discerner's needs render this helpful, the director may invite the discerner to pray through these texts in preparation for enter-ing discernment. These same texts, again according to the director's judgment, may serve during the discernment itself. Directors might present them to discerners during the days and weeks of discernment, abbreviating or amplifying the list according to need.

Discerning the Will of God: An Ignatian Guide to Christian Decision Making (New York: Crossroad, 2009)
This book may be given to the discerner before or during the discern-ment to provide an overview of the process and its elements. It is the companion to the present book. Should the director use the present

book and the discerner this Ignatian title, both will follow the same Ignatian trajectory with the same vocabulary. This Ignatian title will help the discerner grasp more quickly and with less labor the function of the elements and the meaning of the steps in discernment.

Digital Resources

For recorded conferences on discerning God's will, see the following:

frtimothygallagher.org, the "On Disc" tab

discerninghearts.com

iTunes and Google Play; search for "Fr. Timothy Gallagher"

Notes

Introduction

1. Timothy Gallagher, O.M.V., *Discerning the Will of God: An Ignatian Guide to Christian Decision Making* (New York: Crossroad, 2009).

2. See *Spiritual Exercises*, 175–88, where Ignatius describes his three "times" or "modes" of discernment. We will explore these in detail in Chapters 5–9.

3. These writings are the following: the *Spiritual Exercises*, the Ignatian *Directories*, the *Autobiography*, the *Spiritual Diary*, a selection of letters, and the *Constitutions of the Society of Jesus*. All of these are found in Manuel Ruiz Jurado, S.J., ed., *Obras de San Ignacio de Loyola* (Madrid: Biblioteca de Autores Cristianos, 2014). All quotations from the *Spiritual Exercises* are translated by the author. Quotations from the others sources are either translated by the author or cited from existing translations, which are noted each time.

4. Jules Toner, S.J., *Discerning God's Will: Ignatius of Loyola's Teaching on Christian Decision Making* (St. Louis: Institute of Jesuit Sources, 1991); Jules Toner, S.J. *What Is Your Will, O God? A Casebook for Studying Discernment of God's Will* (St. Louis: Institute of Jesuit Sources, 1995).

5. Ignacio Iparraguirre, S.J., ed., *Directoria Exercitiorum Spiritualium (1540–1599)* (Rome: Monumenta Historica Societatis Jesu, 1955), vol. 76. English translation: Martin Palmer, S.J., ed. and trans., *On Giving the Spiritual Exercises: The Early Jesuit Manuscript Directories and the Official Directory of 1599* (St. Louis: Institute of Jesuit Sources, 1996). I will utilize both volumes in this book.

6. I will cite their books and articles as I quote them below.

7. In this book, I will frequently quote sources written in other languages. Unless indicated otherwise, all translations from the original languages are the author's. I have translated these texts in such a way that the language be consistent throughout this book. Thus, for example, Ignatius uses two different words for the three patterns of discernment he describes: "time" ("*tiempo*") and "mode" ("*modo*"). Because in my text I have opted for "mode" as the clearer term for the reader, when the texts cited employ

"*tiempo*," I have translated this as "mode." For the same reason, I have translated "*ejercitante*" ("exercitant") as "discerner," and "election" ("*elección*") as "choice."

8. I list these books and provide a brief description of each in Appendix 4.

9. The formal Spiritual Exercises may be made in the silence of a retreat house for a set number of days, or in daily life by dedicating an hour to prayer each day and meeting with the director weekly over several months. This latter form is often called the "nineteenth-annotation" retreat, a reference to paragraph nineteen of the *Spiritual Exercises* in which Ignatius describes this way of making the Exercises.

10. Ignacio Casanovas, S.J., *Comentario y explanación de los Ejercicios Espirituales de San Ignacio de Loyola* (Barcelona: Editorial Balmes, 1945), II, 231. See also Palmer, *On Giving the Spiritual Exercises*, 305, para. [73]; 310, para. [96].

11. His *Spiritual Diary* provides an example. We will explore this discernment in Chapters 6 and 8.

12. When the experience is taken from a published source, the reference is provided in the corresponding endnote. If no source is named, the experience arose from an interview with the author.

Text

1. *Spiritual Exercises* (hereafter, *SpirEx*) 175–77. Author's translation. For Ignatius's complete text (*SpirEx*, 175–88), and for a note on the translation, see Appendix 2.

Chapter One: Beginning the Discernment

1. In Palmer, *On Giving the Spiritual Exercises*, 254, para. [110]. I have translated "the soul" as "he."

2. See Gallagher, *Discerning the Will of God: An Ignatian Guide*, 18.

3. This touches a fundamental issue for all solidly based discernment: the discerner's image of God. Who is God for the discerner? Is God loving? Merciful? Severe? Quick to condemn? Directors will need to be aware of this and, as necessary, help discerners to embrace an image of God based on God's self-revelation in Jesus.

4. I have utilized the wording of Louis Puhl's translation without his capitalizations: *The Spiritual Exercises*, 72. In order to discern well, therefore, a person must be, in the words of one spiritual director, "morally

mature," that is, free from moral relativism and accepting of the Church's moral teaching.

5. This review is part of the third point in the examen prayer. See Timothy Gallagher, O.M.V., *The Examen Prayer: Ignatian Wisdom for Our Life Today* (New York: Crossroad, 2006), 75–86.

6. One North American spiritual director lists the following among cultural attitudes that may render discernment more difficult today: a "Facebook culture" that desires great numbers of "likes" even from persons not personally known; a culture of entitlement; the need for immediacy that impedes giving time to reflection and desires a quick resolution; the lack of stability in today's culture and so a fear of commitment; an individualism that renders service to others difficult if no benefit to self is perceived.

7. Programs of training for spiritual direction help directors acquire this nonprofessional psychological sensitivity. Additional courses, reading, and online resources may assist directors in gaining this awareness. For a discussion of this issue, see Laurence Murphy, S.J., "Psychological Problems of Christian Choice," *The Way Supplement* 24 (1975): 26–35. Two volumes are devoted to psychology and the Ignatian Spiritual Exercises in the Colección Manresa: *Psicología y Ejercicios Ignacianos*, vols. I and II, nos. 5–6 in the series (Bilbao: Mensajero, 1991).

8. Most likely the second set of rules for discernment would simply confuse these persons at this stage. This second set may be taught later when these persons have reached greater spiritual maturity. See Timothy Gallagher, O.M.V., *Spiritual Consolation: An Ignatian Guide for the Greater Discernment of Spirits* (New York: Crossroad, 2007), 25–29.

9. Palmer, *On Giving the Spiritual Exercises*, 252, para. [100]. See also the Official Directory, Palmer, 323, para. [162].

10. RSVCE, 2nd ed.

11. For a detailed discussion of Ignatian meditation and contemplation, see Timothy Gallagher, O.M.V., *Meditation and Contemplation: An Ignatian Guide to Praying with Scripture* (New York: Crossroad, 2008).

12. Gallagher, *Meditation and Contemplation*, 27–34.

13. Gallagher, *Meditation and Contemplation*, 35–46.

14. Gallagher, *Meditation and Contemplation*, 55–67; *Examen Prayer*, 122–25

15. Gallagher, *Meditation and Contemplation*, 69–72.

16. Gallagher, *Meditation and Contemplation*, 73–76.

17. List of questions in Gallagher, *Meditation and Contemplation*, 73.

18. *SpirEx*, 62, 118, 227.

19. The Official Directory explains: "These repetitions are of great value. It often happens that in an initial meditation upon such matters the understanding is stimulated by their novelty and a certain curiosity. Afterwards, when we abate the activity of the understanding, the way is more open for interior affections, in which the fruit principally consists. In these repetitions, then, we must avoid lengthy processes of thought. We should merely call to mind and briefly run over the matter of our previous meditation, and then dwell upon it with our will and affections." See Palmer, *On Giving the Spiritual Exercises*, 315, para. [126]. John Wickham, S.J., adds: "It is a good practice to encourage those who pray to re-enter their experiences, either in order to pursue them further toward their conclusion, or in order to recognize them more clearly, to 'own' a grace received and thank God for it, or to seek help in responding to it with fidelity. It is all too easy to lose the benefit of graces actually received in prayer. Note that St. Ignatius has built repetitions into the whole structure of his Spiritual Exercises. In general, this is because human beings require time to get hold of their experiences and to respond to them in freedom." See John Wickham, S.J., *Prayer Companions' Handbook* (Montreal: Ignatian Centre Publications, 1991), 34. See also Palmer, *On Giving the Spiritual Exercises*, 169, paras. [40]-[41]; 247, para. [73]; John Veltri, S.J., *Orientations* (Guelph: Loyola House, 1996), vol. 1, 11–14; Miguel Angel Fiorito, S.J., *Buscar y hallar la voluntad de Dios: Comentario práctico a los Ejercicios Espirituales de San Ignacio de Loyola* (Buenos Aires: Ediciones Diego de Torres, 1989), vol. 1, 160–64.

20. A further form of Ignatian prayer is the application of the senses (*SpirEx*, 121–26), essentially a simplified presence in prayer to the grace that has emerged from contemplations and repetitions already made on a scriptural text. This simplified presence permits the grace already received to penetrate more deeply. Regarding the application of the senses, Marian Cowan, C.S.J., and John Futrell, S.J., write: "The method consists in making oneself present to the mystery at the deepest level through interior sight, hearing, touch—all the 'spiritual' senses. Here, as always, different people have different aptitudes and attractions. Some persons are led to interior passivity more through seeing, others through hearing, or another sense, according to the suggestions of Ignatius [122–25]. Some persons focus on detail, while others approach the mystery globally. The great secret is always to make oneself interiorly present to the scene—an opening of one's consciousness into the scene, going right into it and being there simply as an awareness of what is going on. One allows the scene, the words, the actions, the persons contemplated to produce their own effects in the depths of one's heart. Depending upon circumstances, the retreatant will exercise more or

less personal activity during each prayer; but one, finally, must always allow the mystery of Christ to reach to the depths of one's heart to transform it." See Marian Cowan, C.S.J., and John Futrell, S.J., *Companions in Grace: Directing the Spiritual Exercises of St. Ignatius of Loyola* (St. Louis: Institute of Jesuit Sources, 2000), 95. See also Hugo Rahner, *Ignatius the Theologian* (London: Geoffrey Chapman, 1990), 181–213; and Manuel Alarcon, S.J., "Aplicación de sentidos," *Manresa* 65 (1993): 33–46.

21. Gallagher, *Examen Prayer*. See Appendix 4 for a brief description of this book.

22. For these classic five steps, see Gallagher, *Examen Prayer*, 25, 57–102.

23. Gallagher, *Discerning the Will of God: An Ignatian Guide*, 5.

24. I will explain this further in the immediately following section. For a full treatment of these two sets of rules, see my book on each listed in Appendix 4.

25. Ignatius speaks in his rules of the "enemy," "bad spirit," "enemy of human nature," and "bad angel." I will use "enemy" throughout as the word he most commonly uses. See Gallagher, *Discernment of Spirits*, 32–34.

26. See Gallagher, *Spiritual Consolation*, 2.

27. RSVCE.

28. See Gallagher, *Spiritual Consolation*, 40–56.

29. "The *time itself* of the consolation without preceding cause is the time when God draws the dedicated person *'totally in love* of his divine majesty' (*Second Rules*, 2); during this time, the person is *warm* with the *actual* consolation given now by God. The *time following* is the time when the person is no longer warm with an actual consolation without preceding cause given now by God—at this point that consolation is *past*—but *remains* warm with the *favor* and *remnants* of the consolation without preceding cause just concluded" (Gallagher, *Spiritual Consolation*, 117–18). See Chapters 2 and 8 of this book for a complete discussion of consolation without preceding cause.

30. I have modeled this example on the similar one in Gallagher, *Spiritual Consolation*, 121–23.

31. *SpirEx*, 175–88.

32. Chapters 5–9.

33. Official Directory, ch. 22, 1, in Iparraguirre, *Directoria Exercitiorum Spiritualium*, 683. Author's translation, as are all subsequent quotations from this volume. This volume will be cited henceforth as MHSI, 76.

34. Reading, online resources, and training programs abound. Many sources are cited in these notes and in the bibliography. My own include the books listed in Appendix 4 and the digital resources given in the same

appendix. Centers exist throughout North America and elsewhere for the training of spiritual directors in the Ignatian tradition.

35. See Maureen Conroy, R.S.M., *Looking into the Well: Supervision of Spiritual Directors* (Chicago: Loyola Press, 1995).

Chapter Two: Laying the Foundation

1. Palmer, *On Giving the Spiritual Exercises*, 244, para. [63].

2. Palmer, *On Giving the Spiritual Exercises*, 127, para. [45].

3. Palmer, *On Giving the Spiritual Exercises*, 312, para. [105]. See also p. 245, para. [63].

4. See, for example, *SpirEx*, 46, 169, 177, 179, etc.

5. How they do this will depend among other things on how much time is available for the discernment. In some discernments, this may be done without hurry, according to the discerner's need. In others, time may require a briefer review and prayer with the foundation. In either case, the discerner will benefit.

6. *SpirEx*, 23. This translation and all subsequent translations of the *Spiritual Exercises* are the author's, made from the original Spanish of the autograph version of the *Spiritual Exercises*. In translating, I have consulted and occasionally adopted wording from the translations by Louis Puhl, S.J., *The Spiritual Exercises of St. Ignatius: Based on Studies in the Language of the Autograph* (Chicago: Loyola Press, 1951), and Elder Mullan, S.J., *The Spiritual Exercises of St. Ignatius: Translated from the Autograph* (New York: P. J. Kennedy & Sons, 1914). My aim in translating is not elegance of style but rather close adherence to Ignatius's own words.

7. Directory dictated to Juan Alfonso de Vitoria, 21, in MHSI, 76, 101.

8. As indicated above, nor may they be open to any morally bad option.

9. Palmer, *On Giving the Spiritual Exercises*, 149, para. [1]. In the first three points, Polanco uses the third person singular; for the fourth, he adopts the first person plural. I have extended this to all four points. The Latin *indifferentes* is found in MHSI, 76, 329, repeating Ignatius's *indiferentes* in the Spanish original.

10. Many of these are common in Ignatian literature and in the practice of Ignatian spiritual directors; some I have added personally.

11. The quotations are from the RSVCE.

Chapter Three: Removing the Obstacles

1. If these psychological attractions and resistances are strong and deeply rooted, directors may need to suggest counseling. When this suggestion is

made with sensitivity, and if the discerner is open to receive it, great good may result, and the path to solid discernment will be opened.

2. Christine Mugridge and Jerry Usher, *Called by Name: The Inspiring Stories of 12 Men Who Became Catholic Priests* (Westchester, PA: Ascension Press, 2008), 179–80.

3. Jean Vanier, *Community and Growth* (New York: Paulist Press, 1996), 36.

4. Much depends on discerners' image of self and of God. Do they see themselves as loveable in the eyes of others and of God? Is God for them a punishing God, ready to condemn, or a God who loves them and desires to heal human failure and sinfulness (John 3:16; Luke 15)?

5. See Gallagher, *Meditation and Contemplation: An Ignatian Guide to Praying with Scripture*. This short book is dedicated to providing such formation in an accessible way. If time allows, directors might invite discerners to read this book and to pray through the forty scriptural texts outlined for prayer in Gallagher, *An Ignatian Introduction to Prayer: Scriptural Reflections According to the* Spiritual Exercises (New York: Crossroad, 2008). I find that using these two books together, the "textbook" that explains the methods (*Meditation and Contemplation*) and the "workbook" that invites the person to use the methods in actual prayer (*Ignatian Introduction to Prayer*), provides discerners unfamiliar with these methods with the formation in scriptural prayer necessary for discernment.

6. Gallagher, *Meditation and Contemplation*, 55–76.

7. "Above all, we must prepare ourselves for prayer. . . . Anyone who has the right feeling for things which are great and important will, before tackling them, banish distraction and recollect himself inwardly. The same must hold good for prayer—all the more since God, as we have said, is hidden and must be found in faith. Praying is an act of religious worship. The faculty which it must awaken and turn toward the object of worship—if this term may be used—is not merely that of thought and action, but the inmost 'inwardness' of the soul: in other words, the very thing which in man corresponds to the mysterious holiness of God. In everyday life this inner faculty is silent or at best just faintly noticeable, for man is wholly occupied with the worldly aspect of his being, living as it were by his worldly powers. But if prayer is to be true, then that which belongs to the sphere of the holy must come into its own." See Romano Guardini, *The Art of Praying: The Principles and Methods of Christian Prayer* (Manchester, NH: Sophia Institute Press, 1994), 11.

8. Gallagher, *Meditation and Contemplation*, 73–76.

9. In Gallagher, *Examen Prayer* (see Appendix 4), I discuss this prayer in

detail. I believe that directors can do this effectively only if they are themselves praying the examen.

10. *SpirEx*, 44; Official Directory, nn. 134–38, in Palmer, *On Giving the Spiritual Exercises*, 317–18.

11. *Autograph Directory*, [4]; Palmer, *On Giving the Spiritual Exercises*, 7.

12. Among those they may decide to omit might be the following: Gen 3:1–24; Rom 5:12–21; Rom 7:14–25; 1 John 1:5–2:6; Matt 25:31–46; Luke 16:19–31.

13. What constitutes "sufficient" purification in this context? Directors must judge this according to the factors involved in the discernment. Certainly, any firm adherence to sinful behavior, with no sincere desire for change, will hinder discernment. Other factors to be considered include the spiritual and psychological strength or weakness of the discerner, the seriousness of the choice to be discerned, and the time available for the process.

Chapter Four: Forming the Disposition

1. Casanovas, *Comentario*, II, 74.

2. In the full (thirty-day or nineteenth-annotation) Spiritual Exercises made for discerning God's will, suitable candidates already possess or are close to possessing this disposition before they enter the retreat. The directors' task is to assist the maturing of this disposition into final readiness for discernment. In discerning God's will outside the Spiritual Exercises, directors cannot assume that discerners possess this disposition and must guide them toward it. By contrast, however, with directors of the full Spiritual Exercises, these directors generally dispose of more time for this task and, when the time available for discernment allows, may employ the weeks or months necessary for discerners to attain this disposition.

3. Palmer, *On Giving the Spiritual Exercises*, 312, para. [104]. I have translated the Latin *indifferentia* as "availability."

4. Palmer, *On Giving the Spiritual Exercises*, 312, para. [105].

5. *SpirEx*, 16. The following two quotations are from this same paragraph in the *Spiritual Exercises*.

6. See also *SpirEx*, 155 and 157.

7. MHSI, 76, 716.

8. The Official Directory alerts directors to another possibility: "The director should also be aware that a person often enters upon a discernment with excellent dispositions, yet at the actual moment of the discernment some untoward affection arises in him which upsets everything and chokes

the good seed. The director must be circumspect and careful to foresee and head off things of this sort" (Palmer, *On Giving the Spiritual Exercises*, 328, para. [177]).

9. Ignacio Iparraguirre, S.J., *Historia de los Ejercicios Espirituales de S. Ignacio de Loyola,* vol. I: *Práctica de los Ejercicios de S. Ignacio de Loyola en vida de su autor* (Rome: Bibliotheca Instituti Historici Societatis Jesu, 1946), 195. I have translated *inclinación positiva del alma* as a "positive inclination of heart."

10. Palmer, *On Giving the Spiritual Exercises*, 253, para. [105].

11. Summary of an Anonymous Instruction, in Palmer, *On Giving the Spiritual Exercises*, 70, para. [27]. See also Palmer, 254, para. [111], and Toner, *Discerning God's Will*, 95–99. One spiritual director raises the question of attaining the necessary disposition when limited time is available for the discernment, as, for example, when the response to a job offer must be given within a few weeks. In this case, directors will do their best—this is all God ever asks—to help discerners move toward this disposition, and discerners will likewise do their best to seek this grace from God. Such considerations indicate the value of seeking to live constantly in this disposition.

12. Palmer, *On Giving the Spiritual Exercises*, 300, para. [45]. I have rendered "exercitant" as "discerner" and will do so in future quotations from this volume.

13. Official Directory, in Palmer, *On Giving the Spiritual Exercises*, 327, para. [175].

14. Miró, in Palmer, *On Giving the Spiritual Exercises*, 177, para. [83]. See also Palmer, 66, para. [14].

15. Palmer, *On Giving the Spiritual Exercises*, 123, para. [29]. Rather than repeat the word *exercitant* (rendered as "discerner") a second time in the translation, I have followed the Latin original (*in illo*) and translated this phrase "in him." MHSI, 76, 286.

16. Palmer, *On Giving the Spiritual Exercises*, 124, para. [29].

17. Palmer, *On Giving the Spiritual Exercises*, 163, para. [6].

18. MHSI, 76, 153.

19. MHSI, 76, 154.

Chapter Five: Clarity beyond Doubting: The First Mode

1. In discussing the three modes, I will follow the general outline I used in my earlier book, *Discerning the Will of God: An Ignatian Guide*. I do this because I believe the clarity of that presentation serves the present book as well. I do this also because in this way both books may be used

together, the earlier book by the discerner and this book by the director, as they share the process of discernment. My presentation of the modes in this book differs from the former, however, in that here I discuss these modes specifically with regard to the director's role rather than the discerner's. Both in its perspective, therefore, and in the significant additional content required by this change of perspective, the discussion of the modes in this book is new.

2. *Autobiography*, no. 27. Ignatius recounted these events to Luis Gonçalves da Câmara, who later put them in writing. For this reason, da Câmara uses the third person singular ("he was," "he had"). Author's translation.

3. Ignatius uses two words, *time* ("*tiempo*": SpirEx, 175–78; *Autograph Directory*, [6]) and *mode* ("*modo*": SpirEx, 189; *Autograph Directory*, [18]-[19]) for the three ways of discerning God's will described in the *Spiritual Exercises*. The word "time" indicates *when* the spiritual experience described takes place; the word "mode" indicates *how* it takes place. For a developed discussion of these two words as Ignatius uses them, see Toner, *Discerning God's Will*, 102–6. In this book, I will use the second, "mode," as the more immediately accessible of the two. González Dávila speaks also of three *manners* ("*maneras*": MHSI, 76, 516) and Iparraguirre of the *methods* ("*métodos*": *Historia*, I, 205) employed in these three ways of discerning God's will.

4. Emphasis added.

5. Jules Toner highlights these three elements in *Discerning God's Will*, 109.

6. Sampaio writes: "Why did Ignatius give the callings of St. Paul and St. Matthew as examples of the first time of election? In the first place, the two calls are very different: if the call of Paul was unquestionably extraordinary and occurred in a miraculous setting, the call of Matthew took place in the setting of his daily work" (Sampaio, *Los tiempos de elección*, 89). Casanovas adds: "Neither the one [Paul] nor the other [Matthew] made any kind of election; it was given to them already made, and their part was only to follow it 'without doubting or being able to doubt'" (*Comentario*, II, 91).

7. In his *Casebook* of examples, Jules Toner, S.J., describes a similar experience and its justification: "It was not my intention that a preponderance of cases should deal with God's call to a state of life; but the cases which others presented or which I found in print led to this result. And, it must be said, it is these cases that Ignatius had primarily in mind when drawing up his directives for seeking God's will. If one learns to apply his teaching to this primary kind of case for discernment, there should be no problem in applying it to other types of cases." See Toner, *What Is Your*

Will, O God? A Casebook for Studying Discernment of God's Will (St. Louis: Institute of Jesuit Sources, 1995), 3.

8. Luis González Hernández, S.J., suggests that Ignatius's choice of the name "Company of Jesus" for his religious community, and his decision to recount the story of his life to Luis Gonçalves da Câmara may also have been discernments of this kind: *El primer tiempo de elección según San Ignacio* (Madrid: Ediciónes Studium, 1956), 25 n. 28.

9. "The account given here is just as it was written by the person who had the experience. 'Malia' is a pseudonym." Toner, *Discerning God's Will*, 112 n. 14. The account is given on pp. 112–13. I have employed the pseudonym "Anne."

10. First-mode discernment, as in these instances, may be simply given by God outside of any formal process of discernment. It may also be given within a process of discernment in progress. This latter situation is the one Ignatius envisages in his *Autograph Directory*, [18].

11. Sampaio comments on Ignatius's experience regarding the penitential practice: "What is shown to him is so clear that he cannot doubt that it is God who reveals it to him. He can doubt it neither in the moment of the experience itself nor later: his certitude is clear and lasting" (*Los tiempos de elección*, 84).

12. Mark Thibodeaux, S.J., narrates this story in his book *God's Voice Within: The Ignatian Way to Discover God's Will* (Chicago: Loyola Press, 2010), 183–86. The following quotations are taken from these pages.

13. Sr. Margaret Mary of the Sacred Heart, "Vocation story," Passionist Nuns, St. Joseph Monastery, Whitesville, KY, www.passionistnuns.org/vocationstories/AVocationStory/index.htm.

14. See Toner, *Discerning God's Will*, 118–21, and González Hernández, *El primer tiempo*, 109. Both books are excellent sources for further reading on first-mode discernment.

15. *My Brother, the Pope* (San Francisco: Ignatius Press, 2011), 95–96.

16. Casanovas suggests that discerners may humbly pray for the gift of first-mode discernment: "Since this is not the only means that God may use to show his will, no one can expect that he will necessarily experience it; nonetheless, because it is the principal and most sure way, we can ask the Lord for this with all humility, confidence, and constancy" (*Comentario*, II, 94–95). The Official Directory holds the contrary: "But this type of calling is most extraordinary and therefore is neither to be sought from God nor expected" (MHSI, 76, 701). González Dávila expresses the same view: Palmer, *On Giving the Spiritual Exercises*, 255, para. [119].

17. Palmer, *On Giving the Spiritual Exercises*, 137, para. [81].

18. Palmer, *On Giving the Spiritual Exercises*, 255, para. [119].

19. Palmer, *On Giving the Spiritual Exercises*, 329, para. [187].

20. Palmer, *On Giving the Spiritual Exercises*, 329, para. [187]. The commentators are divided on this question. For a review of their positions, see Toner, *Discerning God's Will*, 127–29, and Sampaio, *Los tiempos de elección*, 95–99.

21. Maurice Giuliani, S.J., writes: "Although it is rare, this mode is not reserved only for exceptional cases. Not only among fervent persons and those especially favored by God, but also among beginners we see at times cases in which we can clearly recognize a discernment according to the first mode." See Giulani, "Se decider sous la motion divine," *Christus* 14 (1957): 172. Quoted in Sampaio, *Los tiempos de elección*, 98 n. 85.

22. Mark Thibodeaux, S.J., describes first-mode experiences as "rare," and adds a caution: "It is possible, then, that you the reader will be blessed with such a moment. There may come in an instant the unwavering certainty of what you are called to do. You should note, however, that in my twenty years since entering the Jesuits, I have rarely seen such a thing happen, and I have often witnessed such a *perceived* moment turning out to be untrue" (*God's Voice Within*, 185).

23. Sampaio, *Los tiempos de elección*, 248, quoting González Hernández, *El primer tiempo*, 205.

24. MHSI, 76, 76.

Chapter Six: An Attraction of the Heart: The Second Mode (I)

1. Gallagher, *Discernment of Spirits*, 49. See Chapters 3 and 4 of this book for some parts of my treatment here of spiritual consolation and spiritual desolation.

2. Jacques Maritain, ed., *Raïssa's Journal* (Albany: Magi Books, 1974), 35.

3. *SpirEx*, 316, 317, 322. Having established that the consolation of which he speaks is spiritual, Ignatius does not repeat the adjective each time he speaks of consolation. It is always, however, to be understood when Ignatius speaks of consolation or desolation.

4. See Gallagher, *Discernment of Spirits*, 48–51, for a more detailed discussion of this point.

5. Toner, *What Is Your Will?*, 66. See Gallagher, *Discernment of Spirits*, 59.

6. On the meaning of "good spirit" and "enemy," see Gallagher, *Discernment of Spirits*, 32–35.

7. MHSI, 76, 76: *Autograph Directory*, [18].

8. For this purpose, Ignatius supplies his rules 3 and 4 in *SpirEx*, 316–17. See Gallagher, *Discernment of Spirits*, Chapters 3 and 4, for a discussion of spiritual consolation and desolation as Ignatius describes them in these two rules.

9. See Gallagher, *Discerning the Will of God: An Ignatian Guide*, 83–85.

10. William Young, S.J., trans., in Simon Decloux, S.J., *Commentaries on the Letters and Spiritual Diary of St. Ignatius Loyola* (Rome: Centrum Ignatianum Spiritualitatis, 1980), 134–35. Further details regarding the issue for discernment and Ignatius's process of discernment are available in this and in all editions of the *Spiritual Diary*. To simplify the reading, I have omitted Ignatius's indication of the specific Mass (Holy Trinity, Name of Jesus, Our Lady) he celebrated each day, and the translator's inclusion in brackets of the day of the month: February 3, etc.

11. In *SpirEx*, 147, Ignatius asks the intercession of Mary with her Son, and of the Son with the Father.

12. March 12, 1544. Author's translation, in *Examen Prayer*, 46. The continuation of this quotation is from this same source.

13. Palmer, *On Giving the Spiritual Exercises*, 331, para. [194].

14. *Comentario*, II, 97.

15. See Gallagher, *Discerning the Will of God: An Ignatian Guide*, 88–90.

16. Richard Hauser, S.J., *Moving in the Spirit: Becoming a Contemplative in Action* (Mahwah, NJ: Paulist Press, 1986), 75–76, 79.

17. Note however the vocational discernment of Jerónimo Nadal, S.J., made primarily through spiritual desolation. See Sampaio, *Los tiempos de elección*, 131–32. "Discernment applied to those moments of desolation may be decisive in confirming, by way of opposition, the direction or decision that God desires for the soul. The point that the enemy opposes at all costs is exactly that which God desires" (Sampaio, *Los tiempos de elección*, 132). See also Ruiz Jurado, S.J., *El discernimiento espiritual: Teologia. Historia. Práctica* (Madrid: Biblioteca de Autores Cristianos, 1994), 270.

18. See Gallagher, *Discerning the Will of God: An Ignatian Guide*, 91–92.

19. Association of the Monasteries of Nuns of the Order of Preachers in the United States of America, *Vocation in Black and White: Dominican Contemplative Nuns Tell How God Called Them* (Lincoln, NE: iUniverse, 2008), 24–25.

20. As mentioned earlier (Chapter 1), for Ignatius, the context in all questions of discernment is Church teaching: *SpirEx*, 170.

21. *Catechism of the Catholic Church*, no. 1603, www.vatican.va/archive/ENG0015/__P51.HTM.

Chapter Seven: An Attraction of the Heart: The Second Mode (II)

1. MHSI, 76, 555.

2. Palmer, *On Giving the Spiritual Exercises*, 255, para. [120]. González Dávila specifies: "as found in the first set of Rules for the discernment of Spirits, rules 3–11, and in the directories Doc. 1.11,18." The author astutely identifies these as those rules of the first set in which Ignatius discusses consolation and desolation (rules 3–11), as well as the passages in Ignatius's *Autograph Directory* (first of the directories, nos. 11 [and 12], 18) where he deals with this same topic.

3. *Autograph Directory*, [18], MHSI, 76, 76.

4. *Los tiempos de elección*, 150.

5. *Comentario*, II, 98.

6. See Gallagher, *Discernment of Spirits,* for a commentary on the first set of rules for discernment and *Spiritual Consolation* for a commentary on the second set of rules. As mentioned, space here does not allow me to repeat the full exposition of these rules given in those volumes.

7. "The ability to distinguish accurately between a retreatant whose experience calls for the assistance of the first set of rules and one whose experience calls for the assistance of the second set, is, says Gil, 'one of the most important acts of the one who gives the Spiritual Exercises'" (Gallagher, *Spiritual Consolation*, 139 n. 15).

8. Palmer, *On Giving the Spiritual Exercises*, 336, para. [218].

9. Sampaio, *Los tiempos de elección*, 151. I have translated "soul" ("*alma*") as "person."

10. Official Directory, in Palmer, *On Giving the Spiritual Exercises*, 336, para. [218].

11. "Even though the time of the meditations is the privileged time in which God reveals his will, the directories insist that the signs of God's will may also be given outside the moments of prayer" (Sampaio, *Los tiempos de elección*, 139–40). I have removed the bold type Sampaio uses in this text.

12. Palmer, *On Giving the Spiritual Exercises*, 138, para. [82].

13. Such awareness, as discerners grow in this habit, can become a way of life. David Townsend, S.J., writes: "This might be achieved in many

ways. For instance, at the end of a piece of work or conversation, and before attending to something else, there is frequently room for a quick flash of discerning awareness of God's presence and of the person's own responses to that presence during that piece of work or conversation. There is also frequently time to glance quickly at what is ahead the better to dispose oneself to seek and find God in the new task. This might take a few seconds remaining seated at a desk, or it may take a few minutes walking from one building to another, or it could be done driving to an appointment." See Townsend, *The Examen Re-Examined* (Rome: Centrum Ignatianum Spiritualitatis, 1964), 45. See also Gallagher, *Examen Prayer*, 164. Obviously, the more discerners grow in this practice as an ongoing habit, the more apt they will be to note experiences of spiritual consolation and desolation and perceive their meaning when engaged in second-mode discernment.

14. Sampaio notes that "the elements of the experience [of second-mode discernment] may come prior to the Exercises or be obtained during them" (*Los tiempos de elección*, 146). See also Eusebio Hernández, S.J., in "La elección en los Ejercicios de San Ignacio," *Miscelánea Comillas* 24 (1956), 137. Applied to discernment in daily life, this suggests that directors will wish to ask discerners about any experiences of spiritual consolation or desolation, with their related attractions and resistances to the options in the choice, that may have occurred *before* the discerners approached them for help in discernment.

15. Palmer, *On Giving the Spiritual Exercises*, 302, para. [56].

16. See Gallagher, *Examen Prayer*, 132–35.

17. I find that this helps in several ways. Above all, it seeks from the Lord a grace that both director and discerner need (Matt 7:7). Such prayer also helps both director and discerner to enter the meeting with more peace and greater readiness for the conversation to follow. In addition, it raises the communication to the spiritual level and so helps both director and discerner to speak on this level during the hour. Directors may also wish to close the meeting with a prayer.

18. Simply titled "Short Directory," without the name of an author: MHSI, 76, 443–44. See Palmer, *On Giving the Spiritual Exercises*, 206, para. [16]. I have translated *tyro* ("novice, beginner") as "person."

19. In my exposition I am following Hernández, in "La elección en los Ejercicios de San Ignacio," 138–40.

20. The commentators debate whether or not what Hernandez presents here as a third way of doing second-mode discernment belongs properly to second-mode discernment. See Sampaio, *Los tiempos de elección*, 143–46, for a fine treatment of this issue. The question is whether Ignatius's para-

graph [21] in his *Autograph Directory*, where he speaks of presenting the one option and the other to God on successive days and watching to see "toward which God our Lord gives greater signs of his divine will, like one who presents different foods to a prince and observes which he prefers," pertains to the second or third mode. Some commentators of weight, notably González Dávila (para. [124]) and the Official Directory (para. [195]), understand Ignatius's paragraph [21] as pertaining to second-mode discernment. Sampaio notes, however, that we find nothing in the writings of St. Ignatius to justify an interpretation of paragraph [21] as another way of doing second-mode discernment (p. 144). In fact, in paragraph [21] Ignatius mentions neither consolation nor desolation, the defining characteristics of second-mode discernment. Ruiz Jurado understands paragraph [21], in view of its context in the *Autograph Directory*, as applying not to second-mode discernment but to the second way of doing third-mode discernment (*SpirEx*, 184–87); see Ruiz Jurado, *El discernimiento espiritual*, 275. It must be said that the placing of paragraph [21] after the "last" mode of discernment, that is, the second way of doing third-mode discernment (*Autograph Directory*, para. [20]), renders it difficult to interpret and therefore open to the discussion it has caused. I believe that Sampaio is correct in his conclusion that González Dávila's interpretation of paragraph [21] as pertaining to second-mode discernment is by no means certain ("*discutible*"); see Sampaio, *Los tiempos de elección*, 146. Because, however, I also believe that the alternate presentation of the options as already chosen can be helpful in second-mode discernment, I am following Hernández and the tradition that supports him in viewing this approach as a further way of doing second-mode discernment, without however citing paragraph [21] as its basis. I will cite paragraph [21] explicitly in dealing with third-mode discernment, where I believe this paragraph can also be helpful.

   21. MHSI, 76, 716.

   22. Palmer, *On Giving the Spiritual Exercises*, 135, para. [76].

   23. Palmer, *On Giving the Spiritual Exercises*, 337, para. [221].

   24. Palmer, *On Giving the Spiritual Exercises*, 139, para. [83].

   25. Palmer, *On Giving the Spiritual Exercises*, 281, para. [134].

   26. MHSI, 76, 518. See Palmer, *On Giving the Spiritual Exercises*, 257, para. [129].

   27. Hernández, "La elección en los Ejercicios de San Ignacio," 136. Emphasis in the original. See Sampaio, *Los tiempos de elección*, 152, 198.

   28. See also Ignatius's *Autograph Directory*, [18], where he again describes second-mode discernment as an "experience of consolations and desolations." Palmer, *On Giving the Spiritual Exercises*, 9, para. [18].

29. Thus Polanco: "When the director comes, he should ask an account of these movements. If he detects signs of the good or evil spirit, he should use the Rules for Discerning Spirits, but especially those of the Second Week" (Palmer, *On Giving the Spiritual Exercises,* 138, para. [182]). See also Palmer, 215, para. [78] (Short Directory); 256–57, paras. [123] and [127] (González Dávila); 281, para. [131] (Cordeses); 337, para. [222] (Official Directory).

30. See above, Chapter 1, and, for a full exposition, Gallagher, *Spiritual Consolation.*

31. As the case of Ignatius's discernment between radical and mitigated poverty indicates, the enemy may attempt this tactic later on the spiritual journey as well. Experience confirms the truth of this. On these questions, see Gallagher, *Spiritual Consolation,* 17–29.

32. Even here, however, if discerners are highly attentive to their spiritual experience and if their directors know these rules well in theory and practice, discernment of the enemy's tactic is possible (*SpirEx*, 335). See Gallagher, *Spiritual Consolation,* Chapter 7. As Gil writes, "We find ourselves here at the apex of discernment" (Gallagher, *Spiritual Consolation,* 165 n. 7).

33. Ignatius discusses this aid toward discernment in rules 3 through 7. A separate and important issue is the experience of consolation without preceding cause and how to discern it. Ignatius discusses such consolation in rules 2 and 8 of this second set. Given the practical nature of the present book with its focus on clarity and usability, I have judged it best not to enter this complex issue here. I have treated consolation without preceding cause at length in my book *Spiritual Consolation,* Chapters 2 and 8, to which I refer the reader. Any director who seeks a comprehensive grasp of Ignatius's teaching on discernment must gain familiarity with this matter of consolation without preceding cause and its significance for discernment. This consideration reinforces a point made earlier: through study and experience, directors must pursue a deep understanding of both sets of rules.

34. See Gallagher, *Spiritual Consolation,* 21–22. I have adapted the account for the purposes of this book.

35. Directors will also watch for any experiences of consolation without preceding cause (second set of rules, rules 2 and 8). In my book *Spiritual Consolation,* I expressed my view on how often directors may expect to encounter such experiences: "How frequently may we expect consolation without preceding cause to occur? Ignatius himself does not answer this question, and here, as elsewhere, the commentators are divided. . . . My

own best answer, after years of working in retreat ministry and in spiritual direction, is that consolation without preceding cause does indeed occur in the lives of dedicated people, though not with great frequency. To recognize it when it does appear to have occurred in a person's experience and to assist that person to grasp its meaning, is an invaluable spiritual service. As noted, such spiritual assistance requires a well-prepared and experienced director" (*Spiritual Consolation*, 150 n. 29).

36. See Gallagher, *Spiritual Consolation*, 80–89.

37. In my treatment of second-mode discernment through the application of the second set of rules, I have spoken throughout of a "drawing," that is, of an attraction in time of spiritual consolation toward some choice. Ignatius speaks of the "good and holy thoughts" the enemy brings in times of spiritual consolation: for Patricia, if it is discerned to be of the enemy, this is the "good and holy thought" of serving the refugees; for the pastor, again if it is discerned to be of the enemy, this is the "good and holy thought" of imitating Jesus more fully by serving in an inner-city parish.

38. *Comentario*, II, 476, cited in Sampaio, *Los tiempos de elección*, 150 n. 221.

39. Palmer, *On Giving the Spiritual Exercises*, 258, para. [138].

40. Should directors note an apparent contradiction between the presumed results of a second-mode discernment and what reason sees as evident—a discerner, for example, who clearly does not possess the requisite health judges that through second-mode discernment God has shown him a call to missionary work in the third world—the directors may find it helpful to invite discerners to undertake third-mode discernment as well. On third-mode discernment, see below, Chapters 8 and 9.

41. See Gallagher, *Discernment of Spirits*, 48–51, 60–61.

Chapter Eight: A Preponderance of Reasons: The Third Mode (I)

1. Polanco, in Palmer, *On Giving the Spiritual Exercises*, 139–40, paras. [83] and [85]. See Sampaio, *Los tiempos de elección*, 194.

2. *Comentario*, II, 108.

3. Polanco, MHSI, 76, 314.

4. Casanovas writes: "The ideal of Saint Ignatius was to keep his soul always ready to receive God's visitations and to know how to find these internal visitations, in one form or another, but always leaving the initiative to God whenever he needed to know the divine will in any specific issue." At the same time, Casanovas continues, "He is very rational and consistent

in valuing and seeking the reasons dictated by natural prudence" (*Comentario*, II, 242).

5. For these lists of advantages and disadvantages, see Joseph Munitiz, S.J., and Philip Endean, S.J., eds. and trans., *Saint Ignatius of Loyola: Personal Writings* (London: Penguin Books, 1996), 70–72.

6. See other listings in the following: Simon Decloux, S.J., *The Spiritual Diary of St. Ignatius Loyola: Text and Commentary* (Rome: Centrum Ignatianum Spiritualitatis, 1990), 192–96; Manuel Ruiz Jurado, S.J., ed., *Obras de San Ignacio*, 266–68.

7. *SpirEx*, 178; *Autograph Directory*, [19].

8. José Calveras, S.J., writes: "We must note well that consolations are not excluded from this third mode when the text cited in the Exercises [*SpirEx*, 177] requires that the soul not be agitated by different spirits. The reason is that the free and tranquil exercise of the intellect to ponder the reasons for and against the choices considered is incompatible with interference from thoughts coming from without, which is the work of the different spirits. But such free and tranquil exercise of the intellect is not disturbed but rather aided by consolation, when in the peace and spiritual joy this brings, supernatural light helps the person to discover the true value of the reasons for the greater service of God." See Calveras, "Buscar y hallar la voluntad divina por los tiempos de elección de los Ejercicios de S. Ignacio," *Manresa* 15 (1943): 265.

9. Toner, *Discerning God's Will*, 168.

10. Casanovas, *Comentario*, II, 100.

11. Toner, *Discerning God's Will*, 167. Elsewhere Toner amplifies this list: "such natural powers as attention, memory, foresight, circumspection, understanding, and illation [drawing conclusions from premises]" (*Discerning God's Will*, 171).

12. MHSI, 76, 707.

13. Benigno Juanes, S.J., *La elección ignaciana por el segundo y tercer tiempo* (Rome: Centrum Ignatianum Spiritualitatis, 1980), 113.

14. Pedro de Ribadeneyra, S.J., *Vita Sancti Ignatii de Loyola*, ed. Candido de Dalmases, S.J. (Rome: Monumenta Historica Societatis Jesu, 1965), vol. 93, 739–41. Author's translation in Gallagher, *Discerning the Will of God: An Ignatian Guide*, 105.

15. Gaston Fessard, S.J., *La dialectique des Exercices de Saint Ignace de Loyola*, vol. 1, 78; quoted in Sampaio, *Los tiempos de elección*, 162.

16. *Comentario*, II, 108.

17. See Toner, *Discerning God's Will*, 173.

18. One spiritual director adds, "or perhaps prayerfully considering the three classes of men" (*SpirEx*, 149–57).

19. Juanes, *La elección ignaciana*, 121.

20. Variations of the four columns are possible. Sampaio writes, "In reality, however, are not the disadvantages of taking a decision the same as the advantages of not taking it? Consequently, two columns should be enough, although we see that St. Ignatius uses three columns in discerning the question of income for the churches" (*Los tiempos de elección*, 167 n. 78). Nonetheless, the use of four columns remains the most common practice. Whatever approach the discerner adopts, the advantages and disadvantages of both options must be considered and should be written.

21. I am adapting here to discernment in daily life the counsel of the Official Directory, para. [224]. See Palmer, *On Giving the Spiritual Exercises*, 337. In fact, in the Spiritual Exercises, during the time of election, Ignatius reduces the contemplation of the mysteries of Christ to one rather than two (*SpirEx*, 158–61): the prayer continues, but it is lightened to provide space for the process of election.

22. Sampaio, *Los tiempos de elección*, 296. Again I am adapting a counsel for the formal Spiritual Exercises to discernment in daily life.

23. Palmer, *On Giving the Spiritual Exercises*, 332, para. [201].

24. Sampaio, *Los tiempos de elección,* 167. In this observation, Sampaio echoes Juanes, *La elección ignaciana*, 123. Juanes offers the following example: "Although a person may possess in abundance qualities that permit him to exercise the works of the religious institute to which he considers himself called by God, he should not be advised to enter the institute if his character is such that he will be unable to adapt to the normal conditions of community life."

25. In Thomistic terms, this is to say that third-mode discernment is an exercise of the supernatural virtue of prudence and not natural prudence alone. The virtue of prudence helps us identify and embrace the best means toward the end (goal) desired. In supernatural prudence, the end desired is not simply good health, a successful career, and the like (natural ends), but eternal salvation. Giuliani writes: "Even in this third mode, the decision is an act of supernatural prudence, made in the light of the Holy Spirit." See Maurice Giuliani, S.J., "Se decider sous la motion divine," *Christus* 14 (1957): 180.

26. Palmer, *On Giving the Spiritual Exercises*, 257, para. [131].

27. Palmer, *On Giving the Spiritual Exercises*, 332, para. [202].

28. Palmer, *On Giving the Spiritual Exercises*, 139, para. [83] (Polanco); 179, para. [88] (Miró); 257, para. [131] (Miró); 281–82, para. [137]

(Cordeses). See also Ignatius's Second Directory, a brief collection of counsels given orally: "The exercitant can be told to write down his ideas and movements" (Palmer, *On Giving the Spiritual Exercises,* 13, para. [8]).

29. Palmer, *On Giving the Spiritual Exercises,* 338, para. [225].

30. "*moción racional,*" "*moción sensual.*"

31. Sampaio, *Los tiempos de elección,* 168. Emphasis added.

32. See José Calveras, S.J., *Práctica de los Ejercicios intensivos* (Barcelona: Balmes, 1952), 322. See also Polanco, [84], in Palmer, *On Giving the Spiritual Exercises,* 139. If, Polanco writes, the director sees "that the reflection is proceeding or the will receiving impulses from some false principle or from the admixture of some affection or spirit which is not good, he should warn and instruct him [the discerner] against drawing a bad or false conclusion from bad or false principles, and so making a bad discernment."

33. See Toner, *Discerning God's Will,* 211.

34. John Veltri, S.J., *Orientations,* 2, B (Guelph: Guelph Centre of Spirituality, 1998), 400. One spiritual director suggests the following for this prayer: 1 Samuel 3:10 with its accompanying verses, John 15:16, and the slow repetition of Jesus' prayer in the garden (Matthew 26:39).

35. For these signs, see Toner, *Discerning God's Will,* 210.

36. In his discernment regarding poverty, Ignatius dedicated many days to seeking confirmation. His *Spiritual Diary* chronicles this search in detail.

37. *Discerning God's Will,* 213. In this paragraph, I am following Toner's list of factors given on the page cited.

38. Palmer, *On Giving the Spiritual Exercises,* 141–42, para. [90] (Polanco). The Official Directory follows Polanco's treatment of this issue: Palmer, *On Giving the Spiritual Exercises,* 338–39, paras. [229–32]. My description of the four scenarios utilizes expressions from both. To avoid burdening a text intended for practical use, I will not repeat the reference each time I quote these paragraphs. Interested readers may locate them easily in Palmer's volume on the pages indicated in this note.

39. Palmer, *On Giving the Spiritual Exercises,* 141, para. [90].

40. Polanco: "*a malo spiritu viderentur vel dubio*" (MHSI, 76, 317); the Official Directory: "*viderentur a malo spiritu, vel saltem essent dubiae*" (MHSI, 76, 723).

41. Official Directory: "*voluntas eligentis in suo proposito perseverat*" (MHSI, 76, 723).

42. The director may judge it helpful that Patrick employ the second way of doing third-mode discernment (*SpirEx,* 184–88) as a further verification of his choice. We will consider this option in the next chapter. For a historical example of the first way of doing third-mode discernment, see Palmer,

On Giving the Spiritual Exercises, 352–56. Through this first way, Juan Alonso de Vitoria discerned his Jesuit vocation in 1549.

43. "If the choice is not made in the first or second time [mode], two ways of making it in this third time [mode] are given below" (*SpirEx,* 178). Ignatius repeats this point in his *Autograph Directory:* "When no decision has been taken by the second mode, or one that is not good in the judgment of the one who gives the Exercises (whose task it is to help to discern the effects of the good and evil spirits), the third mode of intellectual discourse according to the six points should be used" (MHSI, 76, 76, *Autograph Directory,* para. [19]).

44. Of this second way of doing third-mode discernment, Ignatius writes: "Lastly, one may use the way that is given after this [first way of third-mode discernment], that is, of four points [second way of doing third-mode discernment, *SpirEx,* 184–88], as the last that may be used" (MHSI, 76, 76, *Autograph Directory,* para. [20]).

Chapter Nine: A Preponderance of Reasons: The Third Mode (II)

1. *Autograph Directory,* [20], in MHSI, 76, 76. In this text, Ignatius describes this second way as consisting of four "points"; in the *Spiritual Exercises,* he describes this second way as consisting of four "rules" (*SpirEx,* 184–87).

2. "The first way is essential to the third mode of discernment; the second way presupposes the first and is merely an aid when the latter is not succeeding, or it can be used to make the conclusion of the first way even more sure" (Toner, *Discerning God's Will,* 183). Ignatius proposes the second way as the last way that may be used after the first way has been tried (*Autograph Directory,* [20]). Subsequent directories go further and propose that the second way should always be used after the first: see Polanco, para. [83] and the Official Directory, para. [223]. This latter text reads: "If the person makes a choice by the first way, he should then weigh it by the second. If the same conclusion results from both, it is a good sign of a good choice" (MHSI, 76, 719). See Sampaio, *Los tiempos de elección,* 296. In discerning his Jesuit vocation (1549), Juan Alfonso de Vitoria employed both the first and second way of the third time (Iparraguirre, *Historia,* I, 259–63; translated in Palmer, *On Giving the Spiritual Exercises,* 352–56).

3. Toner, *Discerning God's Will,* 185. Casanovas understands this first rule as a first manner of doing discernment in the second way: "The first of these rules belongs to a different order than the other three. It is a daugh-

ter of the Principle and Foundation, and assumes that the person is well habituated to see things only in relation to God and to admit in his heart no other love than that of God and of things for God. It further supposes in the person a great facility for seeing at a glance the internal dispositions in which we find ourselves and above all to know the order and path along which this love leads. If then, presuming all of this, I am presented with the choice of a thing toward which St. Ignatius presumes I feel myself inclined, and after a rapid exam of my spirit I can be certain that 'the love that moves me and causes me to choose this thing descends from above, from the love of God, so that I feel first of all in myself that the love, greater or lesser, that I have for the thing I choose is solely for the sake of my Creator and Lord,' I can with full confidence adhere to this inclination or love and follow it and rest in it as in the divine will." Casanovas wisely adds a note of caution: "And I repeat that just as all this is easy and sure in a person who lives the Principle and Foundation, it is equally difficult and dangerous for one who is not habituated to these truths and sentiments of the heart" (*Comentario*, II, 111).

4. Toner, *Discerning God's Will*, 185.

5. Palmer, *On Giving the Spiritual Exercises*, 142, para. [91]. For a parallel text, see the Official Directory, para. [173], in Palmer, *On Giving the Spiritual Exercises*, 327. On this matter, see Sampaio, *Los tiempos de elección*, 173.

6. Toner, *Discerning God's Will*, 185.

7. Toner, *Discerning God's Will*, 185.

8. For this paragraph, see Gallagher, *Discerning the Will of God: An Ignatian Guide*, 114.

9. Toner makes this point in *Discerning God's Will*, 187.

10. Ignatius proposes these three same tests in his Rules for Almsgiving (*SpirEx*, 339–41). My treatment of this fourth rule follows my earlier discussion of it in *Discerning the Will of God: An Ignatian Guide*, 114–15.

11. See Gallagher, *Discerning the Will of God: An Ignatian Guide*, 115.

12. Palmer, *On Giving the Spiritual Exercises*, 139, para. [83].

13. *Comentario*, II, 111. See Sampaio, *Los tiempos de elección*, 171, for other authors who hold similar opinions.

14. Casanovas, *Comentario*, 110: "*una luz más brillante y rápida.*"

15. Toner discusses the understanding of the second way as an intuitive grasp of God's will and argues against this view: "If it were true, there would be no apparent reason for speaking of a second way of the third mode of election rather than a fully distinct fourth mode. What would the so-called second way have in common with the first way of the third mode?"

Toner continues: "There is, it should be noted, a cognitive experience which so resembles intuition as easily to be mistaken for it, and could even be called intuition in a manner of speaking. It is really only an amazingly quick and unreflective form of reasoning on objective data. The third mode of discerning God's will could be carried out in this way by a person who is gifted for such reasoning, but it could be mistaken even by himself as well as by others for an intuition" (*Discerning God's Will*, 190).

16. Mark's story is a real experience shared with his permission. I have changed the external circumstances and have elaborated on some aspects of the director's approach to illustrate Ignatius's counsels for directors.

17. *Autograph Directory*, para. [20]. As indicated, some commentators advise that the second way be employed even when the first seems clear.

18. *Autograph Directory*, para. [20].

19. MHSI, 76, 76, *Autograph Directory*, [21]. See Palmer, *On Giving the Spiritual Exercises*, 9. I have discussed above (Chapter 7 n. 20) the various interpretations of para. [21]. In giving the text and explaining it here, I am simply following Ignatius's own placement of this paragraph after the second way that he has just described as "the last that may be used."

20. In the context of the Spiritual Exercises, the Ortiz brothers suggest presenting the first option in the first hour of prayer, the second option in the second hour of prayer, the first option again in the third hour of prayer, and the second option again in the fourth hour of prayer. In this approach, discerners present both options in alternating fashion within a single day. See Sampaio, *Los tiempos de elección*, 145, n. 200.

21. "*Se podría usar . . .*" (MHSI, 76, 76).

22. Palmer, *On Giving the Spiritual Exercises*, 331, para. [195]. The Official Directory understands this procedure as pertaining to second-mode discernment. See above, Chapter 7 n. 20, and Sampaio, *Los tiempos de elección*, 145.

23. Once again, some commentators suggest that the second way should always be used even when the first way brings clarity.

24. Official Directory, para. [223], MHSI, 76, 719.

Chapter 10: After the Choice

1. Toner, *Discerning God's Will*, 193. Elsewhere Toner adds: "Before entering on discernment of God's will, the only problem facing the person should be that of reaching a judgment. The problem of making a free choice should be firmly settled, so that reaching a judgment of what God wills is *eo ipso* [by that very fact] making a choice of it" (ibid, 78). In terms of the three

acts of Thomistic prudence (counsel, judgment, execution), this is to say that before exploring which option God wills, discerners must already have decided to do it once they will have seen it clearly—that is, that the third act of prudence (execution or command: the actual doing of what has been judged to be God's will) is already decided before reaching the judgment.

2. Official Directory, Palmer, *On Giving the Spiritual Exercises*, 340, para. [240]. Toner writes: "Volitional confirmation is needed after the finalized conclusion of the discernment. Because our will easily falls away from its resoluteness, confirmation of a volitional resolve may be needed for ensuring prompt, energetic, and persevering execution" (*Discerning God's Will*, 193). See also González Dávila, paras. [147]-[148], and the Official Directory, para. [184], in Palmer, *On Giving the Spiritual Exercises*, 260, 329.

3. Weeks Three and Four of the Spiritual Exercises.

4. Palmer, *On Giving the Spiritual Exercises*, 338, para. [227].

5. Palmer, *On Giving the Spiritual Exercises*, 338, para. [227].

6. Palmer, *On Giving the Spiritual Exercises*, 260, para. [149]. González Dávila speaks here of the election in the Spiritual Exercises and so of the week or two dedicated specifically to making a choice. His counsel obviously applies in discernment outside the Exercises as well.

7. Palmer, *On Giving the Spiritual Exercises*, 300, para. [45].

8. Palmer, *On Giving the Spiritual Exercises*, 338, para. [227].

9. In translating, I have adopted occasional wording from Mullan, *The Spiritual Exercises of St. Ignatius of Loyola*.

10. Palmer, *On Giving the Spiritual Exercises*, 338, para. [228].

11. Palmer, *On Giving the Spiritual Exercises*, 92, para. [39]. See the same in Cordeses, in Palmer, *On Giving the Spiritual Exercises*, 282, para. [140]. In para. [141], Cordeses carefully describes a situation in which such vows may be helpful.

12. Iparraguirre, *Historia*, I, 195.

13. Iparraguirre, *Historia*, I, 194–95.

14. Once the discerner has entered the discernment, Iparraguirre writes, the director "should propose the *matter* for the discernment, the helpful *modes* of discernment, and the *way* of approaching it. Once he has done this, the director should leave the person alone with his Creator and Lord. The smallest interference on his part between God and the person would signify the undoing in a moment of the pure and transparent state into which, with so much effort, he has helped the person enter; it would be 'to put his own sickle into the harvest of another,' as St. Ignatius graphically described this to Fr. Vitoria" (*Historia*, I, 195). Ignatius adds that "it is more

suitable and much better, in seeking the divine will, that the Creator and Lord himself communicate himself to the devout soul, inflaming it with his love and praise, and disposing it for the way in which it can better serve him in the future" (*SpirEx*, 15).

15. For a review of this issue, see Sampaio, *Los tiempos de elección*, 229–32, and Toner, *Discerning God's Will*, 251–54. See also Casanovas, *Comentario*, II, 102.

16. *SpirEx*, 175, 178; *Autograph Directory*, [18]-[20].

17. Toner comments: "The evidence for Ignatius's thought on combining the two modes is somewhat ambiguous" (*Discerning God's Will*, 251–52).

18. Thus, for example, González Dávila: "As for the second mode, it is clear that if the soul has reached certainty that the thing is an inspiration or movement from God, it should not wait for further consultation" (Palmer, *On Giving the Spiritual Exercises*, 257, para. [133]); and Cordeses: "If the person concludes the business of the discernment well in the second mode, he can conclude here without going on to the discernment in the third mode, for he is being guided by a better light than that of human understanding" (Palmer, *On Giving the Spiritual Exercises*, 281, para. [132]). On the other hand, Miró writes: "Discernment should normally be made not only in the second but also in the third mode. The one making the discernment in this way will be able to render an excellent account to God, having done in both the second and third mode what lay in his power to learn the will of God" (Palmer, *On Giving the Spiritual Exercises*, 179, para. [87]); and the Official Directory: "Note also that these two methods of the third mode are not only for use in cases where no conclusion has been reached in the second mode. Even if a discernment has already been concluded in the second mode, the third mode contributes to its further confirmation and settling" (Palmer, *On Giving the Spiritual Exercises*, 332, para. [203]).

19. Sampaio, *Los tiempos de elección*, 230.

20. Of Ignatius's use of both modes in his *Spiritual Diary*, Toner writes, "It seems evident that for Ignatius, especially in what he considered a critically important decision, doing his best meant seeking God's will not only energetically and perseveringly but also in all the ways he reasonably could—therefore, by both the second and third modes when these were reasonably possible" (*Discerning God's Will*, 253).

21. Palmer, *On Giving the Spiritual Exercises*, 140, para. [86].

22. Palmer, *On Giving the Spiritual Exercises*, 141, para. [88].

23. Palmer, *On Giving the Spiritual Exercises*, 141, para. [88]. The subsequent quotations are from this same paragraph. The Official Directory

follows Polanco on this issue with slight modifications: Palmer, 333, para. [207].

24. Palmer, *On Giving the Spiritual Exercises*, 282, para. [139].

25. *Autograph Directory*, Palmer, *On Giving the Spiritual Exercises*, 9, para. [22]; *Memoriale*, Palmer, *On Giving the Spiritual Exercises*, 31, para. [12].

26. In Ignatius's language, whether he is called to the "counsels" or the "commandments": *Autograph Directory*, Palmer, *On Giving the Exercises*, 9, para. [22].

27. *Autograph Directory*, Palmer, *On Giving the Spiritual Exercises*, 9, para. [22]. Subsequent directories elaborate on the choices faced by those not called to religious life. Cordeses, for example, writes: "If he chooses the common state of the observance of the commandments, then he must decide whether to do so as a married man or as a cleric [secular priesthood, that is, diocesan priesthood]. If as a married man, then whether with a given office or responsibility or not; if as a cleric, whether with a benefice or not" (Palmer, *On Giving the Spiritual Exercises*, 279, para. [118]). The same principle holds: the discerner is to proceed step by step in the discernment.

28. Among them: Miró, in Palmer, *On Giving the Spiritual Exercises*, 177, para. [81]; de Fabi, in Palmer, 202, para. [28]; Short Directory, in Palmer, 214, para. [73]; González Dávila, in Palmer, 254, para. [112]; Cordeses, in Palmer, 279, para. [115]–[119]; Official Directory, in Palmer, 328, paras. [178]-[182].

29. Palmer, *On Giving the Spiritual Exercises*, 254, para. [112]. For an example of a vocational discernment done according to this sequence, see Palmer, 352–56. In these pages, Juan Alonso de Vitoria describes his discernment in 1549 of his Jesuit vocation. He does this following Ignatius's sequence of choices.

30. Ruiz Jurado, *El discernimiento espiritual*, 276.

31. Toner, *Discerning God's Will*, 297.

32. Toner, *Discerning God's Will*, 299. Elsewhere Toner speaks of a "justifiably certain assent to the conclusion of a discernment" (ibid, 308). Minimally, he writes, this may be expressed as a "concrete practical certainty" (ibid, 315).

33. Toner, *Discerning God's Will*, 70–101.

34. Toner, *Discerning God's Will*, 284. See pp. 274–86 for a detailed treatment of this question.

35. Palmer, *On Giving the Spiritual Exercises*, 254, para. [110]. Cited in Toner, *Discerning God's Will*, 285 n. 21.

36. Palmer, *On Giving the Spiritual Exercises*, 326–27, para. [173]. Cited in Toner, *Discerning God's Will*, 286 n. 30.

37. On doing our best in discernment, see Toner, *Discerning God's Will*, 300–310. He writes: "Doing our best in seeking God's will through a discernment process involves at least the following four factors: (1) learning how to do it as far as our abilities and circumstances make reasonably possible, (2) preparing for and carrying out the discernment in the most favorable external circumstances that are available, (3) getting whatever help from others is needed and available, (4) persevering in the search as long as is reasonable, never concluding quickly merely out of impatience" (ibid., 303).

38. An important qualification of this certitude consists in the limits of discernment that Toner describes in accurate detail: see *Discerning God's Will*, 45–69. Toner writes that "discernment is limited to finding God's will regarding the discerner's own free and responsible choices" (ibid., 51), "is limited to finding God's will regarding choices that the discerner has the right to make" (ibid., 59), and "what God wills actually to happen as consequences of the discerner's decision and free choice is beyond the limits of discernment" (ibid., 62).

39. Toner, *Discerning God's Will*, 62. He continues, "To know what will actually happen in the future is prophetic knowledge and is not needed in order to find and do God's will now." Toner notes that questions of discernment, when formulated with precision, "do not ask whether God wills me to do this or that, but whether he wills me to *choose* to do this or that" (ibid., 66). See pp. 62–69 for Toner's complete discussion of this question. See also John Veltri, S.J., *Orientations*, 2, B, 398.

40. "The concluding judgment to which discernment leads is not that God wills actually to happen that which is projected. It is only an assertion that God wills the discerner to choose the course of action to which the projections point as more for God's glory. What will actually follow is another matter altogether. Whether, therefore, the chosen action will succeed in attaining the concrete goal intended is beyond the reach of discernment" (Toner, *Discerning God's Will*, 63).

41. Sampaio, *Los tiempos de elección*, 179. See also Ruiz Jurado, *El discernimiento espiritual*, 275–76, and n. 187. See also Toner, *Discerning God's Will*, 305–8, for a nuanced discussion of how to proceed when no conclusion has been reached.

Appendices

1. Translation by Louis Puhl, S.J., *The Spiritual Exercises of St. Ignatius: Based on Studies in the Language of the Autograph* (Chicago: Loyola University Press, 1952), 12.

2. In this re-presentation of Ignatius's Principle and Foundation, I have attempted to combine fidelity to the text with accessibility for contemporary readers. I have consulted and occasionally adopted phrases from David Fleming's contemporary renderings of the Principle and Foundation in *Modern Spiritual Exercises: A Contemporary Reading of the Spiritual Exercises of St. Ignatius* (Garden City, NY: Image Books, 1983), 25–26; and *Draw Me into Your Friendship: A Literal Translation and a Contemporary Reading of the Spiritual Exercises* (St. Louis: Institute of Jesuit Sources, 1996), 27.

3. Author's translation in *Discerning the Will of God: An Ignatian Guide to Christian Decision Making*, 141–44. The numbers in parentheses are added to the original; they are standard usage in citing the paragraphs of the *Spiritual Exercises*.

4. In Ignatius's time, a position of ministry granted to members of the clergy that also provided financial support.

5. "There are matters that fall under an unchangeable choice, such as priesthood, marriage, etc. There are others that fall under a changeable choice, such as to accept or relinquish benefices, or to acquire or renounce temporal goods" (*SpirEx*, 171).

6. Author's translation in *Discernment of Spirits*, 7–10.

7. Author's translation in *Spiritual Consolation*, 7–9.

Select Bibliography

I include in this bibliography only the principal Ignatian sources utilized. Full bibliographical details for all other works are given in the endnotes as these are cited.

Early Directories

In the original languages

Iparraguirre, Ignacio, S.J., ed. *Directoria Exercitiorum Spiritualium (1540–1599)*, MHSI, 76. Rome: Monumenta Historica Societatis Iesu, 1955.

In translation

Palmer, Martin, S.J., trans. and ed. *On Giving the Spiritual Exercises: The Early Jesuit Manuscript Directories and the Official Directory of 1599*. St. Louis: The Institute of Jesuit Sources, 1996.

I have used the following directories in this book, all published in both volumes just cited:

Autograph Directory of St. Ignatius

Counsels of Father Duarte Pereyra

Summary of an Anonymous Instruction

Instructions Attributed to Father Paul Hoffaeus

Directory of Father Juan Alfonso de Polanco

Second Directory of Father Diego Miró

Directory of Father Gil González Dávila

Directory of Fr. Antonio Cordeses

The Official Directory of 1599

Writings of St. Ignatius and Commentators

Calveras, José, S.J. "Buscar y hallar la voluntad divina por los tiempos de elección de los Ejercicios de S. Ignacio." *Manresa* 15 (1943): 252–70, 324–40.

———. *Práctica de los Ejercicios intensivos.* Barcelona: Editorial Balmes, 1952.

Casanovas, Ignacio, S.J. *Comentario y explanación de los Ejercicios Espirituales de San Ignacio de Loyola,* vols. I-II. Barcelona: Editorial Balmes, 1945.

Gallagher, Timothy, O.M.V. *Discerning the Will of God: An Ignatian Guide to Christian Decision Making.* New York: Crossroad, 2009.

———. *The Discernment of Spirits: An Ignatian Guide for Everyday Living.* New York: Crossroad, 2005.

———. *The Examen Prayer: Ignatian Wisdom for Our Lives Today.* New York: Crossroad, 2006.

———. *An Ignatian Introduction to Prayer: Scriptural Reflections According to the* Spiritual Exercises. New York: Crossroad, 2008.

———. *Meditation and Contemplation: An Ignatian Guide to Praying with Scripture.* New York: Crossroad, 2008.

———. *Spiritual Consolation: An Ignatian Guide for the Greater Discernment of Spirits.* New York: Crossroad, 2007.

Gil, Daniel, S.J. *Discernimiento según San Ignacio: exposición y comentario práctico de las dos series de reglas de discernimiento de espíritus contenidas en el libro de los Ejercicios Espirituales de San Ignacio de Loyola (EE 313—336).* Rome: Centrum Ignatianum Spiritualitatis, 1983.

Giuliani, Maurice, S.J. "Se decider sous la motion divine." *Christus* 14 (1957): 165–86.

Hernández, Eusebio, S.J. "La elección en los Ejercicios de San Ignacio." *Miscelánea Comillas* 24 (1956): 119–73.

Hernández, Luis González, S.J. *El primer tiempo de elección según San Ignacio.* Madrid: Ediciónes Studium, 1956.

Ignatius of Loyola. *The Autobiography of St. Ignatius Loyola with Related Documents.* Joseph O'Callaghan, trans. New York: Harper & Row, 1974.

———. *Commentaries on the* Letters *and* Spiritual Diary *of St. Ignatius Loyola.* Simon Decloux, S.J., ed. Rome: Centrum Ignatianum Spiritualitatis, 1980.

————. *Obras de San Ignacio de Loyola.* Manuel Ruiz Jurado, S.J., ed. Madrid: Biblioteca de Autores Cristianos, 2014.

————. *The Spiritual Diary of St. Ignatius Loyola: Text and Commentary.* Simon Decloux, S.J., ed. Rome: Centrum Ignatianum Spiritualitatis, 1990.

————. *The Spiritual Exercises of St. Ignatius: Based on Studies in the Language of the Autograph.* Louis Puhl, S.J., trans. Chicago: Loyola University Press, 1951.

————. *The Spiritual Exercises of St. Ignatius of Loyola: Translated from the Autograph.* Elder Mullan, S.J., trans. New York: P. J. Kennedy & Sons, 1914.

Iparraguirre, Ignacio, S.J. *Historia de los Ejercicios Espirituales de S. Ignacio de Loyola,* vol. I: *Práctica de los Ejercicios de S. Ignacio de Loyola en vida de su autor.* Rome: Bibliotheca Instituti Historici Societatis Jesu, 1946.

Juanes, Benigno, S.J. *La elección ignaciana por el segundo y tercer tiempo.* Rome: Centrum Ignatianum Spiritualitatis, 1980.

Ribadeneyra, Pedro de, S.J. *Vita Sancti Ignatii de Loyola.* MHSI, 93. Rome: Monumenta Historica Societatis Jesu, 1965.

Ruiz Jurado, Manuel, S.J. *El discernimiento espiritual: Teologia. Historia. Práctica.* Madrid: Biblioteca de Autores Cristianos, 1994.

Sampaio, Alfredo, S.J. *Los tiempos de elección en los directorios de ejercicios.* Colección Manresa, 32. Bilbao, Santander: Mensajero-Sal Terrae, 2004.

Thibodeaux, Mark, S.J. *God's Voice Within: The Ignatian Way to Discover God's Will.* Chicago: Loyola Press, 2010.

Toner, Jules, S.J. *Discerning God's Will: Ignatius of Loyola's Teaching on Christian Decision Making.* St. Louis: Institute of Jesuit Sources, 1991.

————. *What Is Your Will, O God? A Casebook for Studying Discernment of God's Will.* St. Louis: Institute of Jesuit Sources, 1995.

Veltri, John, S.J. *Orientations,* 2, B. Guelph: Guelph Centre of Spirituality, 1998.

Index of Names

Alarcon, Manuel, S.J., 171

Benedict XVI, Pope, 63

Calveras, José, S.J., 2, 121, 185, 187

Câmara, Luis Gonçalves da, 176, 177

Casanovas, Ignacio, S.J., 2, 42, 43, 76, 92, 107, 110, 116, 133, 137, 168, 174, 176, 177, 184, 185, 188, 189, 192

Conroy, Maureen, R.S.M., 172

Cordeses, Antonio, 2, 91, 100, 147, 183, 191, 192, 193

Cowan, Marian, C.S.J., 170, 171

Dalmases, Candido de, 2, 185

Decloux, Simon, S.J., 179, 185

Endean, Philip, S.J., 185

Fabi, Fabio de, 2, 193

Favre, St. Pierre, 29, 43

Fessard, Gaston, S.J., 185

Fiorito, Miguel Angel, S.J., 170

Fleming, David, 195

Futrell, John, S.J., 170

Gallagher, Timothy, O.M.V., 167, 168, 169, 171, 173, 178, 179, 180, 181, 183, 184, 185, 189

González Hernández, Luis, S.J., 177, 178

Gil, Daniel, S.J., 2, 180, 183

Giuliani, Maurice, S.J., 178, 186

González Dávila, Gil, 2, 9, 15, 26, 46, 64, 92, 100, 108, 120, 143, 148, 149, 176, 177, 180, 182, 183, 191, 192, 193

Hauser, Richard, S.J., 179

Hernández, Eusebio, S.J., 100, 181, 182

Hoffaeus, Paul, 144

Ignatius of Loyola, passim

Iparraguirre, Ignacio, S.J., 2, 45, 144, 167, 171, 175, 176, 188, 191

Juanes, Benigno, S.J., 113, 118, 185, 186

Margaret Mary of the Sacred Heart, Sr., 177

Maritain, Jacques, 68, 178

Maritain, Raïssa, 68, 69

Merton, Thomas, 61

Miró, Diego, 2, 48, 175, 186, 192, 193

Mugridge, Christine, 173

Mullan, Elder, S.J., 172, 191

Munitiz, Joseph, S.J., 185

Murphy, Laurence, S.J., 169

Nadal, Jerónimo, S.J., 179

Palmer, Martin, S.J., 167, 168, 169, 170, 172, 174, 175, 177, 178, 179,

Complete List of Titles by Timothy Gallagher, O.M.V.

Praying the Liturgy of the Hours
A Personal Journey
Paperback, 112 pages, ISBN 978-0-8245-2032-8
Also available in eBook format

Begin Again
The Life and Spiritual Legacy of Bruno Lanteri
Paperback, 358 pages, ISBN 978-0-8245-2579-8
Also available in eBook format

A Reader's Guide
The Discernment of Spirits
An Ignatian Guide for Everyday Living
Paperback, 104 pages, ISBN 978-0-8245-4985-5

Meditation and Contemplation
An Ignatian Guide to Praying with Scripture
Paperback, 112 pages, ISBN 978-08245-2488-3
Also available in eBook format

Spiritual Consolation
An Ignatian Guide for Greater Discernment of Spirits
Paperback, 192 pages, ISBN 978-0-8245-2429-6
Also available in eBook format

The Crossroad Publishing Company

Which Ignatian title is right for you?
Timothy Gallagher, O.M.V.

Tens of thousands of readers are turning to Fr. Gallagher's Ignatian titles for reliable, inspirational, and clear explanations of some of the most important aspects of Christian spirituality. Whether you're a spiritual director, priest, or minister, longtime spiritual seeker, or beginner, Fr. Gallagher's books have much to offer you in different moments in life.

◆ When you need short, practical exercises for young and old: *An Ignatian Introduction to Prayer*
Group leaders who are looking for practical exercises for groups, including groups who may not have much experience in spiritual development, will want to acquire *An Ignatian Introduction to Prayer: Scriptural Reflections According to the Spiritual Exercises.* This book features forty short (two-page) Ignatian meditations, including Scripture passages, meditative keys for entering into the scriptural story, and guided questions for reflection. These exercises are also useful for individual reflection both for experienced persons and beginners: beginners will recognize and resonate with some of the evocative passages from Scripture; those familiar with Ignatian teaching will appreciate the Ignatian structure of the guided questions.

◆ When your life is at the crossroads: *Discerning the Will of God*
If you are facing a turning point in life, you know how difficult it can be to try to hear God's will amid the noise of other people's expectations and your own wishes. Ignatius

The Crossroad Publishing Company

of Loyola developed a series of exercises and reflections designed to help you in these times so that your decision can be one that conforms to God's will for your life. *Discerning the Will of God: An Ignatian Guide to Christian Decision Making* is a trustworthy guide to applying those reflections to your own particular circumstances. This guide, which does not require any prior knowledge of Ignatian spirituality, can be used by people of any faith, though some elements will be more directly applicable to Catholic readers.

◆ When you want classic spiritual discipline to apply every day: *The Examen Prayer* and *Meditation and Contemplation*

Individuals wanting to deepen their prayer lives using a spiritual discipline will find *The Examen Prayer* an important resource. The examen prayer is a powerful and increasingly popular resource for finding God's hand in our everyday lives and learning to be receptive to God's blessings. This easy-to-read book uses stories and examples to explain what the examen is, how you can begin to pray it, how you can adapt it to your individual life, and what its benefits for your life can be. Highly practical!

Because *The Examen Prayer* draws from the experiences of everyday life, it can stand on its own as a guide to the prayer of examen. Those looking to begin their practice of meditation and contemplation, which for Ignatius is always based on Scripture, may choose their own Scripture passages or draw from the forty examples in *An Ignatian Introduction to Prayer,* mentioned earlier.

A second favorite is *Meditation and Contemplation: An Ignatian Guide to Praying with Scripture.* Anyone familiar with Ignatian spirituality has heard about meditation and contemplation. In this volume, Fr. Gallagher explains what is unique to each practice, shows how you can profit from

The Crossroad Publishing Company

both at different times in your spiritual life, and reveals some of the forgotten elements (such as the preparatory steps and colloquy) and how the structure can be adapted to your particular spiritual needs.

♦ When you're ready to move more deeply into Ignatian thought: *The Discernment of Spirits* and *Spiritual Consolation*

Spiritual directors, directees, and others who want to understand the deeper structures of Ignatian thought have come to rely on *The Discernment of Spirits: An Ignatian Guide to Everyday Living,* and *Spiritual Consolation: An Ignatian Guide for the Greater Discernment of Spirits. The Discernment of Spirits* leads us through Ignatius's Rules for discernment, showing both their precise insight into the human soul and their ability to illustrate the real-life struggles of spiritual seekers today. As Fr. Gallagher writes, his practical goal is "to offer an experience-based presentation of Ignatius's rules for discernment of spirits in order to facilitate their ongoing application in the spiritual life. This is a book about living the spiritual life." Because it forms the foundation for so many other aspects of Ignatian thought, *The Discernment of Spirits* has become Fr. Gallagher's best-selling book and has been the basis for a TV series.

Spiritual Consolation extends this same approach, interweaving stories and principles for a more profound understanding of Ignatius's Second Rules for discernment.

Support your local bookstore or order directly from the publisher at www.crossroadpublishing.com
To request a catalog or inquire about quantity orders, e-mail sales@crossroadpublishing.com

The Crossroad Publishing Company

About the Author

Father Timothy M. Gallagher, O.M.V. (frtimothygallagher.org), was ordained in 1979 as a member of the Oblates of the Virgin Mary, a religious community dedicated to retreats and spiritual formation according to the Spiritual Exercises of Saint Ignatius. He obtained his doctorate in 1983 from the Gregorian University. He has taught (St. John's Seminary, Brighton, MA; Our Lady of Grace Seminary Residence, Boston, MA), assisted in formation work for twelve years, and served two terms as provincial in his own community. He has dedicated many years to an extensive ministry of retreats, spiritual direction, and teaching about the spiritual life. Fr. Gallagher is the author of nine books (Crossroad) on the spiritual teaching of Saint Ignatius of Loyola and the life of Venerable Bruno Lanteri, founder of the Oblates of the Virgin Mary. He currently holds the St. Ignatius Chair for Spiritual Formation at St. John Vianney Theological Seminary in Denver.

About the Publisher

The Crossroad Publishing Company publishes CROSSROAD and HERDER & HERDER books. We offer a 200-year global family tradition of books on spiritual living and religious thought. We promote reading as a time-tested discipline for focus and understanding. We help authors shape, clarify, write, and effectively promote their ideas. We select, edit, and distribute books. Our expertise and passion is to provide wholesome spiritual nourishment for heart, mind, and soul through the written word.